ASPEN PUBLISHERS

Practicing Persuasive Written and Oral Advocacy

Case File IV

David W. Miller
Professor of Law, Emeritus
University of the Pacific
McGeorge School of Law

Mary-Beth Moylan
Assistant Director, Appellate Advocacy, and Lecturer in Law
University of the Pacific
McGeorge School of Law

George Harris
Professor of Law (on leave)
University of the Pacific
McGeorge School of Law

Wolters Kluwer
Law & Business

AUSTIN   BOSTON   CHICAGO   NEW YORK   THE NETHERLANDS

Aspen Publishers
Attn: Permissions Department
76 Ninth Avenue, 7th Floor
New York, NY   10011-5201

To contact Customer Care, e-mail customer.care@aspenpublishers.com,
call 1-800-234-1660, fax 1-800-901-9075, or mail correspondence to:

Aspen Publishers
Attn: Order Department
PO Box 990
Frederick, MD 21705

Printed in the United States of America.

1 2 3 4 5 6 7 8 9 0

ISBN 978-0-7355-6422-0

ISSN 1539-4603

About Wolters Kluwer Law & Business

Wolters Kluwer Law & Business is a leading provider of research information and workflow solutions in key specialty areas. The strengths of the individual brands of Aspen Publishers, CCH, Kluwer Law International and Loislaw are aligned within Wolters Kluwer Law & Business to provide comprehensive, in-depth solutions and expert-authored content for the legal, professional and education markets.

CCH was founded in 1913 and has served more than four generations of business professionals and their clients. The CCH products in the Wolters Kluwer Law & Business group are highly regarded electronic and print resources for legal, securities, antitrust and trade regulation, government contracting, banking, pension, payroll, employment and labor, and healthcare reimbursement and compliance professionals.

Aspen Publishers is a leading information provider for attorneys, business professionals and law students. Written by preeminent authorities, Aspen products offer analytical and practical information in a range of specialty practice areas from securities law and intellectual property to mergers and acquisitions and pension/benefits. Aspen's trusted legal education resources provide professors and students with high-quality, up-to-date and effective resources for successful instruction and study in all areas of the law.

Kluwer Law International supplies the global business community with comprehensive English-language international legal information. Legal practitioners, corporate counsel and business executives around the world rely on the Kluwer Law International journals, loose-leafs, books and electronic products for authoritative information in many areas of international legal practice.

Loislaw is a premier provider of digitized legal content to small law firm practitioners of various specializations. Loislaw provides attorneys with the ability to quickly and efficiently find the necessary legal information they need, when and where they need it, by facilitating access to primary law as well as state-specific law, records, forms and treatises.

Wolters Kluwer Law & Business, a unit of Wolters Kluwer, is headquartered in New York and Riverwoods, Illinois. Wolters Kluwer is a leading multinational publisher and information services company.

Contents

INTRODUCTION

Case File IV is the fourth in the series, *Practicing Persuasive Written and Oral Advocacy*. The case is based on *M.F. et al. v. Chancery Court et al.*, a lawsuit commenced in the Mississippi Chancery Court for Van Buren County as a petition for a second-parent adoption. The details of the story are described in this introduction and in the materials that make up the case file.

The case file can be used for numerous issues including subject matter jurisdiction, Eleventh Amendment immunity, substantive due process, and equal protection. These issues are detailed in the introduction, but can be further explored and expanded by individual professors and classes in their use of the materials. In fact, in light of new case law in Connecticut and Massachusetts allowing same-sex couples to legally marry, an issue of comity could be infused into the problem by adding details of an out-of-state marriage license.

The Story

The petition of Marissa Franco to adopt her same-sex partner's daughter was denied by the Chancery Court after a detailed report by the Mississippi Department of Human Services found that the adoption would be in the best interest of the child, but that the Department was constrained to recommend adoption by Mississippi Code § 93-17-3(5), a statute that expressly prohibits adoption by same gender couples. The Chancery Court relied not only on the Mississippi Code in its denial of the petition for adoption, but also on independent findings that were inconsistent with the findings made by the Department of Human Services. Plaintiffs took an appeal to the Chancery Court decision in state court, and simultaneously brought a federal court action alleging that the Mississippi Code violated their due process and equal protection rights and that the Chancery Court decision was arbitrary and capricious under state law. The state court stayed the appeal pending resolution of the federal claims.

The underlying facts of the story provide a human element to the current hot legal and social issue concerning same-sex marriage and parenting. In the story, Marissa Franco and Claire Whitney are a couple raising their two daughters together as a family. They were married in their church, but the State of Mississippi does not recognize same-sex marriage.

Claire Whitney is the adopted mother of Karina Giles, the child that Marissa Franco seeks to also adopt. The family believes adoption of Karina by Marissa Franco is necessary because Claire Whitney, a university professor and the primary breadwinner in the family, has been diagnosed with multiple sclerosis and will likely suffer increasingly debilitating effects of the disease. Marissa Franco will need full parental rights to take care of Karina in the event of Claire's debilitation or death.

Marissa Franco's petition for adoption is denied because a Mississippi law expressly prohibits couples of the same gender from adopting. There is no question that adoption would otherwise be in Karina's best interest.

Structure and Theory of Case File IV

Case File IV contains litigation documents that can be used to support problems and assignments concerning a number of challenging legal issues, including immunity, constitutional due process and equal protection clauses, and subject matter jurisdiction. The documents are created specifically for teaching written and oral advocacy. While they are not "real" court documents, we have aimed to make them realistic and easy to use. The file contains the complaint, answer, motions, supporting declarations, and underlying documents that support the litigation. Orders by the court and additional evidentiary materials are available in the Teacher's Manual and can be divulged or withheld at appropriate times in the course of the problem.

Exercises using these materials may consist of between one and three memoranda and oral arguments before the trial court, as well as briefs and oral arguments before a court of appeal. Because the problem contains support for two constitutional challenges, one substantive due process theory and the other equal protection, it can be divided over the course of two years with two different sets of students.

The Teacher's Manual that supports this Case File provides ideas for assignments, research files, and the court opinions. Included in the Teacher's Manual are bench briefs that relate to the various memoranda briefs that can be assigned using the materials, and additional exhibits that can be added to the problem to increase the complexity of the legal analysis.

The case *M.F. et al. v. Chancery Court* is set in a fictitious United States District Court because the federal rules of practice are consistent across jurisdictions and are easily accessible to most law students. A full record is developed in the trial court so that students can learn to argue both legal and factual issues, pore over the record to identify issues, determine the relevance of facts, find evidentiary support for their positions, and understand the challenge of working with witness declarations. The record is also useful at the appellate level because it can be used to demonstrate the application of the standard of review and to teach students the importance of raising all key issues in the trial court. The case is designed to culminate in the appellate court, rather than the Supreme Court of the United States, because advocacy before a court of appeals is a typical experience for litigators. Additionally, from a teaching perspective the role of precedent is much more significant at the court of appeals level. Encouraging students to use case authority effectively is a crucial component of persuasive written and oral advocacy. A setting in the court of appeals facilitates this goal.

Uses of Case File IV

These materials were created to support an innovative required course in Appellate Advocacy at the University of the

Pacific, McGeorge School of Law.[1] In that course, which is a full year required second-year class, each student writes two memoranda in the trial court, orally argues those motions, writes an appellate brief, and argues the appeal. In addition, one of the memoranda is revised for an additional graded assignment, and students complete ungraded written work, research exercises, editing exercises, and standard of review exercises. Students' practical exercises are supported by lectures and weekly workshops. Students also read from the text Fontham, Vitiello & Miller, *Persuasive Written and Oral Advocacy in Trial and Appellate Courts* (Aspen 2007).

Although this Case File was created with that year-long course in mind, it can also support shorter courses in Legal Research and Writing, Legal Process, Persuasive Writing, Pre-Trial Practice, and Moot Court. The Teacher's Manual suggests how faculty can use these materials for a variety of courses and teaching objectives.

For ease of use over time, all dates are adjustable. "YR-00" refers to the year in which you are using the book. "YR-01" means one year earlier. Thus, if you are using the book in 2009, "YR-01" means 2008, "YR-02" means 2007, and so forth.

If you find any inconsistencies or incoherence in Case File IV, please let us know. Mary-Beth Moylan is the managing agent for the Case File series now. She may be reached at (916)-739-7223 or by email at mmoylan@pacific.edu. We hope you enjoy working with Case File IV.

M.B.M.
D.V.M.
G.H.

---

[1]The course now is entitled Appellate and International Advocacy and we have incorporated at least one international or transnational legal issue into our problems for the last three years. Look for future Case Files to contain this globalized perspective.

IN THE CHANCERY COURT
FOR VAN BUREN COUNTY
22ND CHANCERY DISTRICT
STATE OF MISSISSIPPI

```
22nd CHANCERY DISTRICT
FILED
August 13, YR-01
VAN BUREN COUNTY, MISSISSIPPI
```

In re: The Adoption of a Child   )
As Described in the Petition,   )   Petition for Adoption
By Marissa Franco, Petitioner   )   No. A–YR-01–532

The petition of Marissa Franco respectfully shows:

1.   That your petitioner, who was born on August 18, YR-30, in Chattanooga, Tennessee, is a single woman who resides in Van Buren County, State of Mississippi, and has so resided for in excess of 90 days preceding the filing of this petition.

2.   That the petitioner is desirous of adopting Karina Giles (hereinafter referred to as "Karina"), a female child who is 11 years of age, having been born on June 6, YR-11, in the City and County of San Francisco, California.

3.   That the petitioner is informed and believes that Karina's natural mother was Abigail Resnick (hereinafter referred to as "Abigail"), who was born on January 11, YR-43, and died on October 7, YR-08.

4.   That the petitioner is informed and believes that Karina's natural father is Dustin Giles (hereinafter referred to as "Dustin"), who was born on August 30, YR-53; that Abigail and Dustin were married on July 9, YR-15, in the City and County of San Francisco, California, and were divorced on November 23, YR-11, by order of the Sacramento County Superior Court in Sacramento, California; and that in or about January, YR-10, Dustin abandoned his daughter, Karina, and has had no contact with either Karina or any of the adults who have had custody of Karina since that time. Dustin's whereabouts are unknown to the petitioner and are unable to be determined by reasonable efforts.

5.   That the petitioner is informed and believes that from about YR-10 until the

time of Abigail's death, Abigail lived in a committed life partnership with Claire Whitney (hereinafter referred to as "Claire"), who was born on July 5, YR-50; that on or about April 7, YR-08, Claire adopted Karina pursuant to a decree of adoption entered by the Sacramento County Superior Court in Sacramento, California; and that the decree of adoption did not terminate Abigail's parental rights.

6.   That the petitioner is informed and believes that in August of YR-07, following Abigail's death, Karina moved with Claire, her adoptive mother, to Bristol, Mississippi, in the County of Van Buren. They have since continuously resided in Van Buren County.

7.   That the petitioner and Claire have lived together in Bristol since June of YR-06, and on March 13, YR-05, they solemnly committed themselves to each other in a service of commitment at All Saints Episcopal Church, in Bristol. Since June of YR-06, and continuing to the present, the petitioner and Claire have participated equally in the parenting of Karina.

8.   That in YR-04, Claire was diagnosed with a debilitating disease that has recently progressed to the point where Claire is confined to a wheelchair and needs assistance in several daily life functions, such as dressing herself.

9.   That it would be in Karina's best interest to be adopted by the petitioner so as to insure continuity of parenting in the event of Claire's increasing disability and eventual death.

10.   That Claire consents to Karina being adopted by the petitioner as long as her own rights and responsibilities as Karina's adoptive parent are in no way impaired or diminished.

11.   That Karina has expressed her willingness to be the adoptive child of both Claire and the petitioner.

12.   That the petitioner is able properly to bring up and furnish Karina with suitable nurture and education.

13.   That there are attached to this petition the following documents:

EXHIBIT A - An affidavit verifying the allegations of the petition and consenting to petitioner's adoption of Karina, executed by Claire Whitney, Karina's adoptive parent;

EXHIBIT B - A consent to this adoption executed by Magdalena Resnick, Abigail's only living next-of-kin within the third degree;

EXHIBIT C - A certificate from Harold Savoy, M.D., attesting to Karina's physical and mental condition;

EXHIBIT D - A sworn statement of all property owned by Karina.

WHEREFORE your petitioner prays for a decree of this court that the said Karina Giles shall, from and after the date of the decree, be deemed the child of the petitioner, and for such other relief as to this court may seem fit and proper according to law.

Respectfully
submitted,

Marissa Franco
Marissa Franco

Natalie Moldonado
Natalie Moldonado, Esq.

485 Court Street
Lofborough, MS 38706
Telephone: (756) 922-3828
State Bar No. 111285

Attorney for Petitioner

Dated: August 13, YR-01

JURAT[1]

State of Mississippi   )
County of Van Buren   )   SS

Before me, a Notary Public in and for the state and county aforesaid, this day personally appeared the within named petitioner, Marissa Franco, who says that she has read the foregoing petition and the exhibits thereto and that the matters therein averred of her own personal knowledge are true; and that averments based on information and belief are based on credible information coming to her which she believes to be true.

Given under my hand and official seal, this 12th day of August, YR-01

NOTARY
SEAL

Elaine Plummer
Elaine Plummer

My Commission Expires on May 12, YR+01.

---

[1]A "jurat" is the clause written at the foot of an affidavit, stating when, where, and before whom the affidavit was sworn. BLACK'S LAW DICTIONARY 990 (Rev. 4th ed. 1968). To save space, the jurat of each succeeding document in this case file will not be spelled out. –Ed.

EXHIBIT A

AFFIDAVIT OF CLAIRE WHITNEY

Claire Whitney, being first duly sworn, deposes and says:

1. I am the Claire Whitney ("Claire") who is referred to throughout Marissa Franco's petition to adopt Karina Giles.

2. I am personally acquainted with all the facts averred in the petition, except the date and place of Marissa's birth, as alleged in the first paragraph, and I hereby verify that all those facts are true to the best of my knowledge and belief.

3. I am deeply devoted to my adopted daughter, Karina Giles, and want nothing but the best for her.

4. Since Marissa has been living with me and Karina, she has shared equally in the parenting of Karina. Marissa is a warm and loving person. She and Karina obviously care very much for each other. Marissa and I get along very well in co-parenting Karina. In the event that something should happen to me that would make me no longer able to care for Karina, I can think of no better outcome than that Marissa be able to carry on as Karina's mother. And even while I am still able to care for Karina, there are many reasons why it would be advantageous for Marissa to be one of Karina's parents, such as acceptance at Karina's school and parental recognition in the event that Karina should need to be hospitalized.

5. My doctors tell me that my prognosis is very uncertain. Multiple Sclerosis is an unpredictable illness. My own abilities to carry on the normal functions of everyday life have varied tremendously. There is no number of months or years that can be meaningfully assigned as my life expectancy. I want to live a long time to see Karina grow up. Her best opportunity to grow up healthy and well-adjusted is under the joint parenting of me and Marissa. If I do not live a long time, there is no better arrangement for Karina's upbringing than that Marissa adopt her and thus be able to continue parenting her without interruption.

6. I enthusiastically consent to Marissa's adoption of Karina on one condition: that being that the decree of adoption have no effect on my status as one of Karina's adoptive parents. My consent is not and should not be construed as an abandonment or renunciation of Karina as my child. On the contrary, it is because I firmly believe that it is in Karina's best interests to have another parent in addition to myself, and that other

parent should be Marissa. If terminating my status as Karina's adoptive parent is the only way to allow Marissa to adopt Karina, with great regret I must withhold my consent.

7. As to Karina's property, she has no property other than clothing and personal belongings. However, she is the beneficiary of a trust which is described in Exhibit D.

Respectfully submitted,

Claire Whitney
_____
Claire Whitney

JURAT [omitted]

EXHIBIT B

<u>AFFIDAVIT OF MAGDALENA RESNICK</u>

Magdalena Resnick, being duly sworn, deposes and says:

1. I am the sister of Abigail Resnick Giles, who is referred to in paragraphs 3-6 of Marissa Franco's petition to adopt Karina Giles.

2. I am 40 years of age and live in Casper, Wyoming.

3. Abigail and I had no siblings. Our parents are both deceased. Both of our parents were only children. Thus, I am Karina's only living natural relative within the third degree of kinship according to the civil law system.

4. I freely and voluntarily consent to Karina's being adopted by Marissa Franco, so that Karina will have two adoptive parents. Allowing this adoption to take place, but without calling Claire Whitney's adoptive parenthood of Karina into question, is definitely in Karina's best interest.

Respectfully submitted,

Magdalena Resnick
_____
Magdalena Resnick

JURAT [omitted]

EXHIBIT C

HEALTH CERTIFICATION

Elodia Stern-Campbell, M.D.

Bristol Pediatric Center

125 Oak Avenue

Bristol, MS 38705

August 2, YR-01

TO WHOM IT MAY CONCERN:

I practice pediatric medicine in Bristol, MS. I am licensed to practice medicine in the states of Massachusetts, Mississippi, Minnesota, and Wisconsin. I earned my M.D. degree at the the University of Kansas Medical School and did my internship and residency in pediatrics at the Mayo Clinic in Rochester, MN. I have had several years of postdoctoral education and clinical training at Children's Hospital in Boston, MA. I am a diplomate of the National Academy of Pediatric Medicine, the highest level of certification for pediatric physicians. Pediatric medicine specializes in the medical care, diagnosis, and treatment of children and younger adolescents.

I first saw Karina Giles, dob June 6, YR-11, on November 17, YR-06, when she was five years old. She was brought to my office by her mother, Claire Whitney, for a routine checkup and inoculations. (I was told that Karina and her mother had only recently moved to Bristol. The mother said that Karina had received regular well-baby care where she previously lived, although I do not have her medical records prior to my first seeing her.) Since then, I have seen Karina approximately every 6 to 8 months for well-child examinations and four times in connection with routine sicknesses and injuries. In addition to examining her, I have watched her interactions with adults, including mainly her mother.

I most recently saw Karina today. On this occasion she weighed 76 pounds and stood 55 inches tall, which are on the small side of average, but within the normal ranges for her age. Her temperature, pulse and blood pressure were unremarkable. Clinical examination of her head, eyes, ears, mouth, throat, neck, chest, abdomen, limbs, skin, and orifices were all negative. Results of vision and hearing tests were unremarkable. According to her mother, she sees a dentist regularly.

My overall impression of Karina is that she is a normally developed, intelligent, socially mature, and healthy pre-pubescent girl. She has no congenital abnormalities. She has no chronic diseases. She has been treated by me only for routine childhood illnesses, such as colds, flu, and strep throat, and for an occasional minor injury.

I have discussed parenting with Karina's mother, Claire Whitney, and the mother is well informed about safe and healthy child-rearing practices, nutrition, and childhood development.

If I may be of further assistance in evaluating this child, please do not hesitate to contact me.

E. Stern-Campbell, M.D.

Elodia Stern-Cambell, M.D.

EXHIBIT D

AFFIDAVIT OF KWAME DUNCAN

Kwame Duncan, being duly sworn, deposes and says:

1. I am a senior trust officer for the Bank of J. M. Wilkinson, a private bank and trust company in Sacramento, CA. I am familiar with the financial affairs of the late Abigail Resnick and of the arrangements that were made to support her daughter, Karina Giles.

2. At the time of her death, Abigail Giles left an estate that was valued at about $185,000.00. She left a simple will leaving everything to Karina. In consultation with Karina's surviving adoptive mother, Claire Whitney, and the executor of Abigail's estate, Magdalena Resnick, all of Abigail's property was liquidated and the proceeds were put in trust for the benefit of Karina. The Bank of J. M. Wilkinson was named as the trustee and continues to serve in that capacity.

3. Under the terms of the trust, after expenses have been paid, current income is paid monthly on Karina's behalf to Claire Whitney. The monthly payment has averaged between $615 and $620 per month. The trustee has discretion to invade principal for the purpose of paying extraordinary medical, educational and other necessitous expenses. To date, it has not been necessary to make any payments from principal.

4. When Karina attains the age of 18, income payments will begin being made directly to her. Between the ages of 21 and 36, the principal will be paid to Karina in annual installments until the principal is exhausted and the trust terminates.

5. The trust has grown modestly since YR-08. The latest principal balance is $202,593.69.

Respectfully submitted,

Kwame Duncan

Kwame Duncan

JURAT [omitted].

```
              IN THE CHANCERY COURT
              FOR VAN BUREN COUNTY
              22ND CHANCERY DISTRICT
              STATE OF MISSISSIPPI
```

```
            22nd CHANCERY DISTRICT
                  FILED
              August 22, YR-01
           VAN BUREN COUNTY, MISSISSIPPI
```

In re: The Adoption of a Child)
As Described in the Petition,   )   No. A-YR-01-532
By Marissa Franco, Petitioner   )

REFERRAL FOR INVESTIGATION AND STAY OF PROCEEDINGS

WHEREAS the petition for adoption in this case was filed on August 13, YR-01; and

WHEREAS the court has inadequate information about the petitioner, her family, her home, and the child, to make the determinations required by law to be made in a case of adoption.

THEREFORE, it is by the court ordered that:

1.   The file in this case shall be referred to the Mississippi Department of Human Services (hereinafter referred to as "the Department");

2.   The Department shall conduct an investigation, including, but not limited to, a home study, pursuant to Miss. Code Ann. § 93-17-11, as amended;

3.   The Department shall report to the court concerning the child, giving the material facts upon which the court may determine whether the child is a proper subject for adoption by the petitioner, whether the petitioner is a suitable parent for the child, whether the proposed adoption is in the child's best interest, whether the answers to the foregoing questions are impacted by the fact that the child resides with both the petitioner and the child's adoptive mother, and any other facts or circumstances that may be material to the proposed adoption;

4.   The investigation shall be conducted and the report shall be prepared at the petitioner's sole expense, and at no cost to the state or county, in satisfaction of which the petitioner

shall pay directly to the Department pursuant to Miss. Code Ann. § 93-17-12, as amended, a fee of One Thousand Dollars ($1,000.00) on or before August 29, YR-01;

5.   The Department shall file its report with this court, with copies to the petitioner, to the attorney for the petitioner, and to all other interested parties and their attorneys, if any, on or before March 1, YR-00; and

6.   All further proceedings in this matter are hereby STAYED until March 1, YR-00, or until the filing of the Department's report, whichever first occurs.

IT IS SO ORDERED.

Dated: August 22, YR-01

Lucas Rhodes
Lucas Rhodes, Chancellor
Van Buren County

IN THE CHANCERY COURT
FOR VAN BUREN COUNTY
22ND CHANCERY DISTRICT
STATE OF MISSISSIPPI

22nd CHANCERY DISTRICT
FILED
March 1, YR-00
VAN BUREN COUNTY, MISSISSIPPI

In re: The Adoption of a Child)
As Described in the Petition,) No. A–YR-01–532
By Marissa Franco, Petitioner)

REPORT OF THE MISSISSIPPI DEPARTMENT OF HUMAN SERVICES

The Mississippi Department of Human Services presents its report on the petition of Marissa Franco to adopt Karina Giles. This matter was referred to the Department on August 22, YR-01, by the Chancery Court for Van Buren County, and was subsequently assigned to the Division of Children and Family Services. The investigation and preparation of this report were assigned to Laura Tran, MSW, LCSW. This report was reviewed and approved by the Director of the Division of Children and Family Services, Kelsey Cameron, MSW.

I. The Child

Karina Giles, a female, was born on June 6, YR-11, in Sacramento, California, and her birth was duly registered in that City. She was delivered vaginally and there were no complications. She has no genetic or other chronic diseases, and her health history is unremarkable. She is of superior intelligence, and she consistently works at or above her grade level at school.

Karina's birth mother is now dead. Her birth father lost contact with the family in YR-10 and has been unable to be located despite diligent efforts.

Karina was adopted by Claire Whitney in Sacramento, California, by a court decree dated April 7, YR-08, which was during the lifetime of the birth mother. This was a co-parent adoption, which did not terminate the birth mother's parenthood, as permitted by California law.

Claire Whitney moved with Karina to Bristol, Mississippi, in Van Buren County, sometime in August, YR-07, after the death of Karina's birth mother. Claire Whitney and the petitioner, Marissa Franco, have been sharing living quarters and responsibility for parenting Karina since June of YR-06. Marissa filed the instant petition to adopt Karina on August 13, YR-01, when

Karina was 10 years of age.

II. Information Regarding the Birth Parents

Karina's birth mother was Abigail Giles (née Resnick). She was 29 years old when Karina was born. She was a graduate of both college and law school and had been engaged in the practice of law for two years when Karina was born. Abigail reduced her work hours to about half time after the child's birth. From then until Abigail's death, Karina was parented about half time by Abigail and about half time by others, including a nanny and, later on, Claire Whitney. According to all reports, Abigail was a loving and responsible parent. There are no indications of genetic diseases in her family, and she suffered from no chronic diseases or disabilities during her lifetime.

Karina's birth father was Dustin Giles, who was 40 years old when Karina was born. Investigation disclosed no employment history for Dustin Giles. He supported himself from his income as an independent investor. There are no indications that Dustin played any significant role in parenting Karina. There are some indications that Dustin was an alcoholic, although this could not be conclusively determined. Despite the Department's diligent efforts, no other genetic or health history was obtained regarding Dustin.

About a year before Karina was born, Abigail and Dustin began having problems in their marriage. Apparently Dustin's drinking was a source of friction. Before Karina was born, her birth parents entered marriage counseling with Claire Whitney, Ph.D., a licensed clinical psychologist in Sacramento.

The Department interviewed Dr. Whitney, but she felt constrained not to reveal much about her counseling of Abigail and Dustin. It is clear, however, that Dustin resisted the counseling process, while Abigail did not. In fact, it appears that a rather strong bond developed between Abigail and Dr. Whitney.

Dustin moved out of the family home in Sacramento on March 27, YR-11. He moved back in for the last month of Abigail's pregnancy and was present for Karina's birth. Abigail and Dustin terminated counseling with Dr. Whitney in July of YR-10. Dr. Whitney was unwilling at that time to continue counseling Abigail separately. On November 23, YR-11, Dustin and Abigail were divorced. Less than two months later, Abigail and Claire Whitney became lovers. It appears that this was Abigail's first lesbian experience, whereas Claire reports that she has regarded herself as a lesbian since adolescence.

In May of YR-10, Abigail and Karina moved into Claire's home in Elk Grove, California, a suburb of Sacramento. Along about the same time, Claire cut back her practice hours to about half time, and thereafter, she and Abigail participated about equally in caring for Karina. About six months later, Abigail and Claire jointly petitioned for a co-parent adoption of Karina, which was granted by the California court on April 7, YR-08, when Karina was almost three years old. From reports of people (mostly former neighbors and professional colleagues) who knew Abigail and Claire at this time, they were both excellent parents who gave Karina a happy and healthy home life.

On October 7, YR-08, Abigail was killed in a vehicular collision. Karina grieved her mother's death very deeply, but not excessively. Her ability to withstand this loss and to go through a normal grief process was greatly aided by Claire, who was both a professionally trained psychologist and a warmly loving adoptive mother to Claire.

III. Information Regarding the First Adoptive Parent

Claire Whitney is now 49 years old. She attended college in California and obtained her Ph.D. in clinical psychology from Northwestern University in Chicago, Illinois. She interned in various settings, and in YR-17, after obtaining her California license to practice as a clinical psychologist, she commenced private practice in Sacramento. The Department has discussed Dr. Whitney with several of her professional colleagues, and she is held in the very highest regard as a skilled and effective clinician and a generous and good-hearted person.

Claire has no history of genetic or chronic diseases prior to YR-04, and she has been in generally good health for nearly all her lifetime.

Claire "came out" as a lesbian while in college. She has had four serious and long-lasting love relationships with women since then. She also has spent significant parts of her adult life as celibate and not in relationship. She enjoys warm friendships with both men and women. She does not display any behaviors, mannerisms, or styles that would stereotype her as having a particular gender orientation.

Claire has never been married and is childless. She has several nieces and nephews to whom she is close. In addition, she had children as clients when she worked as a clinical psychologist. She manifests excellent understanding of child development, the responsibilities and challenges of parenting, and effective parenting techniques.

After Abigail's death, Claire reexamined her career goals and decided to give up clinical work in favor of an academic position. In the spring of YR-07 she was offered and accepted an appointment as an Assistant Professor of Psychology in the graduate program at Bristol University in Bristol, MS. She and Karina moved to Bristol in August of YR-07, and she took up her new position shortly after that.

During the first months of her work as a professor, Claire employed an au pair and occasional child sitters to care for Karina. Karina appears to have been stressed by the great changes in her life, and for several months she displayed transitory regressive behaviors.

Claire's situation changed in February, YR-06, when Claire met Marissa Franco.

IV. Information Regarding the Prospective Adopting Parent

Marissa Franco is 29 years old, having been born on August 18, YR-30, in Chattanooga, Tennessee. Both her parents were circus performers, her father as a clown and her mother as an aerialist. They lived a peripatetic lifestyle. Neither of her parents were well-educated. However, they appear to have had a stable marriage and to have been loving parents to Marissa. Marissa was their only child. The circumstances of Marissa's upbringing meant that she had much less structure and predictability than most children.

Marissa's schooling was erratic. During most winter months, her parents stayed in Chattanooga, and she attended public schools there. However, she and her parents continued traveling with the circus for several weeks after public schools customarily open in the fall, and she was withdrawn from school several weeks before the end of most school years. At the beginning and end of most school years, she attended many and various public schools throughout the United States until she quit school and left home at the age of 15. Marissa never earned very good grades in school, although she never failed either. She tested as being of superior intelligence with a mild learning disability. Her greatest interest was art, and she has been painting, sculpting, and welding inspired works of art since she was in sixth grade.

There is no evidence of genetic diseases in Marissa's family background. She has not suffered from any chronic diseases except for chronic ear infections up until age 8. She seems to have had more than her fair share of colds, migraine headaches, and other transitory disorders. In the past five years, however, she reports that her health has been excellent.

Marissa lived as a vagrant for two years after she left home. She reports that during this time she regularly indulged in alcohol and marijuana and was sexually promiscuous with both men and women. Also during this time, she got pregnant and gave birth to her daughter, Isabel, on October 5, YR-13, when Marissa was 17 years old. After Isabel's birth, Marissa settled down. She found employment as a waitress in Big Bay, Michigan. She and Isabel lived in a tiny trailer home. In YR-09, she became acquainted with R.T., a prominent judge. He recognized her great artistic talent and encouraged her to complete her GED and enroll in a first-rate art school, which she did.

Marissa first came to Bristol, Mississippi, in August of YR-07 to accept a full scholarship and enroll as an art major at Bristol University, which has a nationally recognized fine arts department. She graduated from Bristol University in YR-03, and has since established a private studio in Bristol. Her work has gained sufficient recognition and popularity that she is able to pay rent on her studio and support herself and Isabel. In YR-02, her net income was $41,293, all of which was derived from selling her art.

Marissa and Claire met in January, YR-06, at a gallery open house in Bristol featuring Marissa's sculpture and paintings. Claire has collected paintings for many years, and she was attracted to Marissa's work. Marissa and Claire soon became fast friends and, not long afterwards, lovers. Marissa has always regarded herself as bisexual. She has not been sexually promiscuous since about a year after Isabel was born.

Marissa and Isabel moved in with Claire and Karina in June YR-06. Marissa and Claire share living expenses and parenting responsibilities for the children. Both have flexible work schedules, so that the girls rarely need to be cared for by anyone other than Marissa and Claire. In May YR-05, they sealed their lifelong commitment to each other in a commitment ceremony at All Saints Episcopal Church in Bristol.

Marissa is a very good parent. She lacks the academic understanding of children possessed by Claire, but she has an intuitive sense of children's needs. She is playful, humorous, and optimistic and the children always seem happy in her presence. While her late adolescent life includes many examples of extreme irresponsibility, there is every indication that Marissa is now a very responsible person. Her financial affairs appear to be well-managed, her studio is remarkably orderly, and by her own report and Claire's, she has never done anything inappropriate or foolish in taking care of the children.

V. Living Circumstances

In April YR-04, Claire was diagnosed with multiple sclerosis. Her disease has progressed rather rapidly. Like most people with MS, Claire has had her ups and downs, with the downs predominating. Within the last year, however, her condition seems to have stabilized under the influence of new medications. As of the time of the Department's home study, Claire was confined to a wheel chair and needed help with dressing. She is intellectually bright and vibrant. Her speech is only slightly impaired. Claire continues to meet all of her teaching and other responsibilities at the University.

Claire continues to play an equal role with Marissa in parenting the girls. However, Claire and Marissa have decided that the girls should no longer be left alone for extended periods with Claire, lest Claire's limitations impair her ability to insure the safety of the children in case of an emergency. Marissa has moved her studio into their home and now spends much more time at home than previously. They are currently building a sizeable addition to the home in order to accommodate both Marissa's need for a larger studio and the family's need for more space with growing children.

Claire's physicians are unable to state a definite prognosis for Claire. Until very recently MS was a fatal disease. However, newer treatments are beginning to demonstrate signs that the lives of persons with MS may be able to be extended considerably. The unstable nature of Claire's illness makes it impossible to predict whether she will die this year or live another 30 years.

Both Claire and Marissa are extremely concerned about the potential impact of Claire's illness on Karina. They think it is important that both Claire and Marissa be legally recognized as parents to Karina so that either of them can perform all of the responsibilities of parenthood without interruptions caused by Claire's illness.

The home is owned by Claire, but she intends in the near future to convert title to a joint tenancy with Marissa. The structure is a two-story, single family dwelling with about 3,000 square feet of living space. It has four bedrooms. One bedroom is used as Claire's study. Another has recently been converted to Marissa's studio. Karina and Isabel share a bedroom. When the addition to the home is completed, Karina and Isabel will return to having separate bedrooms. The dwelling is in very good condition, showing no signs of deferred maintenance. The yard is tidy and the inside of the house is clean and neat. The furniture is somewhat sparse, but sufficient for the family's needs. The kitchen and pantry are well stocked with the ingredients and implements needed for healthy eating. (Marissa now does most of the cooking, although the girls are eager to learn, Marissa is teaching them.) The home is equipped with all appropriate fire and safety devices, and the girls are regularly instructed on safety issues both at home and away from home. Both girls have sufficient clothing in good repair.

The girls treat each other as sisters and each of the adult women in the household as parents. They both realize that their living situation is unusual, but they claim to think nothing of it. They both have age and gender appropriate attitudes towards males and females and their gender roles in society.

Both Karina and Isabel attend Harriet Tubman Middle School, a public school in Bristol. Karina is in 5th grade and Isabel is in 6th grade. They both have good school records, with no conduct problems and adequate or better academic progress. Karina struggles some with arithmetic and mathematics, otherwise school work seems to come easily to her. Karina is an excellent writer, and some of the stories that she shared with the Department's investigator showed great wit and imagination, and excellent writing skills for her age. Examination of her school record and interviews with her teachers disclosed no problems at school. Karina appears to be well-liked by her teachers and her peers.

Both children receive regular medical and dental care and health screening provided in school.

VI. Other Children and Family Members

Neither Marissa nor Claire has other children. Marissa's parents are still living and in good health. Claire has only one living relative, a sister, who lives in Wyoming. No one other than the two women and the two daughters live in the home.

VII. Financial Situation

Marissa's income, although modest, is adequate for herself and her daughter, Isabel. It would be difficult for her to support another child independently. However, the trust fund that was established for Karina following the death of her birth mother is more than adequate for Karina's needs. According to the trustee, the principal of the fund is now worth about $200,000. The trustee regularly disburses slightly in excess of $600 per month for Karina's benefit.

Claire earns $65,000 per year as a professor and owns property worth about $425,000. She owns the home in which she, Marissa, and the girls reside, and is well able to afford the monthly mortgage payment, utilities, and taxes. In the event of her death, her current will would place all of her assets in trust for the benefit of Karina, Marissa, and Isabel.

VIII. References

Four local references have recommended Marissa favorably as an adoptive parent.

IX. Consents

No consents from the birth parents are required. Karina's birth father abandoned her many years ago and cannot be located. Karina's birth mother is deceased. Her only other living blood relative within the third degree is her aunt, Magdalena Resnick, who has signed a written consent to Marissa's adoption of Karina.

The only other person from whom consent might be required is Claire Whitney, Marissa's adoptive parent. She has signed a written consent to Marissa's adoption of Karina, but only on the condition that her consent does not result in the termination or diminution of her rights as an adoptive parent.

X. Findings and Recommendation

Karina Giles is a bright, normal, healthy 11-year old girl. She has lived through many changes during her short life, including her parents' divorce, her mother's taking up with a female lover who eventually adopted Karina, her mother's death, and, most recently, her adoptive mother's move from California to Mississippi and her taking up with another female lover. Despite all these changes, Karina's homes have consistently been warm, supportive, and loving. She has had the benefit of excellent parenting from her birth mother, her adoptive mother, and the petitioner.

If Claire Whitney should pass away any time during the foreseeable future, Karina's best interests would be served by her remaining with Marissa in the same household as Isabel, with Marissa being legally recognized as her parent. Even while Claire is still alive, it is often necessary for Marissa to assume the parental role for Karina and the outside world.

Marissa's ability to assume that role would be greatly facilitated if Marissa were legally recognized as one of Karina's parents. The cohesiveness of the family would be enhanced if both of the adults in the children's lives were of equal status. The Department expresses no opinion as to the applicability and effect of the 2000 amendment to Alabama Code sec. 93-17-3, which prohibits "adoption by couples of the same gender." Absent contrary legal guidance, the Department would regard Marissa's current petition as involving an adoption "by an unmarried adult" rather than a couple.

For the foregoing reasons, the Department finds that the adoption of Karina Giles by Marissa Franco would be in Karina's best interests and recommends that the adoption be approved.

Respectfully submitted,

Laura Tran

Laura Tran, MSW, LCSW

Reviewed and approved,

Kelsey Cameron

Kelsey Cameron, MSW, MPA
Director, Div. of Children & Family Services
Mississippi Department of Human Welfare

Dated: March 1, YR-00

```
                  IN THE CHANCERY COURT
                  FOR VAN BUREN COUNTY
                  22ND CHANCERY DISTRICT
                  STATE OF MISSISSIPPI
```

```
In re: The Adoption of a Child)
As Described in the Petition, )      No. A-YR-01-532
By Marissa Franco, Petitioner )
```

DENIAL OF PETITION FOR ADOPTION

WHEREAS the petition for adoption in this case was filed on August 13, YR-01; and

WHEREAS, on August 22, YR-01, the Petition was referred for investigation and report by the Mississippi Department of Human Resources and further proceedings in this matter were stayed until the report was submitted or March 1, YR-00, whichever first occurs;

WHEREAS, on March 1, YR-00, the Mississippi Department of Human Resources submitted its report;

WHEREAS the Attorney General of the State of Mississippi requested permission to participate as amicus curiae in support of the application of Miss. Code Ann. § 93-17-3(5)in the briefing and arguing of the final decree in this case, to which petitioner's counsel did not object;

WHEREAS petitioner's counsel, Natalie Moldonado, Esq., and counsel for the Attorney General's Office, Landon Carney, Esq., submitted written memoranda and oral arguments on the issue of whether this court should follow the findings and recommendation of the Mississippi Department of Human Resources; and

WHEREAS the court has fully and carefully considered the Department's report as well as the arguments of counsel, and is now ready to rule;

THEREFORE, it is by the court ordered, adjudged and decreed that the Petition for Adoption should be DENIED for the reasons set forth in the following memorandum.

MEMORANDUM

The petition asks the court to sanction the adoption of K.G., an eleven-year-old girl by two lesbians, one a 49-year-old psychologist and college professor whose adult life has been marked by serial lesbian relationships; the other, a 29-year-old "artist" who ran away from home when she was 16, and admits that thereafter she was sexually promiscuous with both men and women, abused drugs, and got pregnant out of wedlock when she was only 17. For this court to countenance the proposed adoption of K.G. (1) would not be in the best interests of the child, (2) would be contrary to the declared public policy of the State of Mississippi, and (3) would violate § 93-17-3(5) of the Mississippi Code.

(1) The interests of a child are rarely served by being adopted by a homosexual couple. There is reason to believe that the outcomes of homosexual adoptions are generally less successful than the outcomes of adoptions by heterosexual couples. The Department of Human Resource's report depicts the petitioner and her lesbian lover as being responsible people, but the report fails to address the issue of their homosexual lifestyle and the morality of their living situation. The burden of proving that a proposed adoption would be in the best interests of the child is upon the petitioner. The report addresses the best interests of the child from a very narrow perspective and fails to dispel the court's concerns.

The petitioner grew up in a very unhealthy environment. She ran away from home as a teenager and lived a life of sexual debauchery and drug use. While she claims to have cleaned up her act, it appears from the report that she has done so under the influence of older and more stable persons. The petitioner is 20 years younger than K.G.'s adoptive mother, who is a professional person with an advanced degree. It appears the petitioner depends on older role models who have influenced her for keeping up the appearance of stability in her life. However, one of the major justifications offered for this proposed adoption is that K.G. will need the petitioner after her adoptive mother has passed away. There is no assurance in this record that the petitioner's life style will remain as stable once her older and more mature role model has left the scene.

Petitioner's sole income is from her earnings as an artist. Artists' incomes are notoriously unstable. Petitioner's financial situation would be greatly improved if she could gain control over K.G.'s trust fund. It would a topsy turvy world in which an adoption would be granted on the grounds that it would be in the financial best interests of the adoptive parent.

(2) While the law may countenance certain aspects of the homosexual life style, see <u>Lawrence v. Texas</u>,539 U.S. 558 (2003), neither morality nor public policy must bow to the homosexual agenda. Our court of appeals has clearly indicated that homosexuality is a highly relevant and negative consideration in issues of child custody. <u>S.B. v. L.W.</u>, 793 So.2d 656 (Miss. Ct. App. 2001). A fortiori, should that be true for proposed adoptions.

(3) Section 93-17-3 of the Mississippi Code was amended in 2000 to add: "Adoption by couples of the same gender is prohibited." The petitioner argues that her petition does not request adoption by a "couple" but only by an "unmarried adult," as is permitted. However, the reality is that this petition was motivated by the needs of a couple in a situation where one of them has become ill. If petitioner's analysis were followed, homosexual couples could evade the intent of the law by subjecting a child to two "unmarried adult" adoptions, rather than an outlawed single "couple adoption."

For the foregoing reasons, the petition for adoption is denied.

IT IS SO ORDERED.

Dated: June 29, YR-00   *Lucas Rhodes*
                                           Lucas Rhodes, Chancellor
                                           Van Buren County

IN THE
UNITED STATES DISTRICT COURT
FOR THE MIDDLE DISTRICT OF MISSISSIPPI

M.F., K.G., by her next friend, C.W., and C.W. on her own behalf,
 	
             Plaintiffs
 	
        vs.
 	
CHANCERY COURT OF VAN BUREN COUNTY, MISSISSIPPI; LUCAS RHODES, individually and in his official capacity as Chancellor of the Chancery Court for Van Buren County, Mississippi; CODY ELLISON, individually and in his official capacity as Director of the Mississippi Department of Human Services; and TOMMY FENDER, individually and in his official capacity as Attorney General of the State of Mississippi,
 	
           Defendants
	))

Civil Action No. *YR*-00-
3975

UNITED STATES DISTRICT
COURT
FILED
July 24, *YR*-00
MIDDLE DISTRICT OF MISSISSIPPI

COMPLAINT FOR DECLARATORY AND INJUNCTIVE RELIEF
(CIVIL RIGHTS VIOLATION)

Introduction

1. Officials of the State of Mississippi denied the application of M.F., an adult

citizen of Mississippi, to adopt K.G., an 11-year-old child who for five years has been

part of a joint family headed by M.F. and K.G.'s subsisting adoptive parent, C.W. The

denial was ordered despite a finding by the Mississippi Department of Public Welfare that

the proposed adoption would be in K.G.'s best interest. The reasons for this action were

(A) an addition to Mississippi law in the year 2000, which declares that "adoption by couples of the same gender is prohibited," Miss. Code Ann. § 93-17-3(5), and determinations by the Mississippi Attorney General, the Director of the State Department of Human Services, and the Chancery Court of Van Buren County, Mississippi, that this unconstitutional statute should prohibit M.F. from adopting K.G., and

(B) a purported finding by the Chancery Court of Van Buren County that the adoption would not be in K.G.'s best interest—despite well-supported contrary findings by the Department of Human Services—based on the Chancellor's subjective preconceptions about the "homosexual lifestyle."

2.   M.F., K.G., and C.W. bring this action pursuant to 42 U.S.C. § 1983, for a declaratory judgment that—

(A) Mississippi's prohibition of single-gender couple adoptions so impairs the plaintiffs' protected liberty and privacy interests as to constitute a denial of substantive Due Process of Law;

(B) Mississippi's prohibition of single-gender couple adoptions so discriminates in the availability of an important legal privilege between persons who are members of same-gender couples and all other persons, without any adequate countervailing state interest, as to constitute a denial of equal protection of the laws; and

(C) the Chancellor's finding about K.G.'s best interest, based on the Chancellor's ideas about "the homosexual lifestyle," is so lacking in evidentiary support as to be insufficient under Mississippi law to support the denial of M.F.'s meritorious petition to adopt K.G.

Jurisdiction

3.　Counts 1 and 2 of this action are based on 42 U.S.C. § 1983. This court has subject matter jurisdiction over those counts pursuant to 28 U.S.C. §§ 1331 and 1343(3). Count 3, based on Mississippi law, is part of the same case or controversy as Counts 1 and 2, and is thus within this court's supplemental jurisdiction pursuant to 28 U.S.C. § 1367(a).

The Parties

4.　The plaintiffs are all citizens of Mississippi. K.G. is an 11-year old girl whom M.F. wishes to adopt so as to become K.G.'s co-parent with C.W., who is K.G.'s sole adoptive parent by virtue of a decree of adoption entered by the Superior Court of Sacramento County, California. M.F. and C.W. have been co-parenting K.G. for five years, and both desire the proposed adoption to take place.

5.　The defendant Chancery Court of Van Buren County, Mississippi, is the court that, acting under color of state law, denied M.F.'s petition to adopt K.G.

6.　The defendant Lucas Rhodes is the Chancellor of the Chancery Court of Van Buren County, Mississippi, who, acting under color of state law, entered the order denying M.F.'s petition to adopt K.G.

7.　The defendant Cody Ellison is the Director of the Mississippi Department of Human Services, which thoroughly and impartially investigated the proposed adoption of K.G. by M.F., concluded that the proposed adoption was in K.G.'s best interest, but nonetheless, acting under color of state law, recommended to the Chancery Court that the proposed adoption be denied because Miss. Code Ann. § 93-17-3(5) prohibits adoptions by couples of the same gender.

8. The defendant Bobby Fender is the elected Attorney General of the State of Mississippi, whose responsibilities include enforcement of the laws of the State of Mississippi, and who, acting under color of state law, advised the Department of Human Services that it must recommend against M.F.'s being allowed to adopt K.G. despite the Department's finding that the adoption would be in K.G.'s best interest.

Common Facts

9.   K.G. was born June 6, YR-11, in Sacramento, CA. Her birth mother was A.G. Her birth father was D.G. A.G. and D.G. were divorced on November 23, YR-11.   D.G. subsequently abandoned K.G., and his whereabouts are unknown.

10. After A.G.'s divorce, A.G. and C.W. began living together in a committed relationship. On April 7, YR-08, C.W. adopted K.G. by order of the Superior Court of Sacramento County, California. This was a co-parent adoption under the laws of California, and it did not abrogate A.G.'s status as K.G.'s parent. It did, however, terminate D.G.'s parental rights.

11. Six months later, A.G. was killed in a car crash. This tragic event would have left K.G. an orphan but for the fact that C.W. had previously adopted K.G., thus leaving C.W. as K.G.'s sole surviving parent.

12. In YR-07, C.W. moved with K.G. to Bristol, Mississippi, to take up her new career as a member of the psychology faculty at Bristol University.

13. C.W. met M.F. shortly after arriving in Bristol. Four months later, C.W. invited M.F. and her daughter, I.F., to share living quarters with C.W. and K.G. M.F. was a single mother, and I.F. and K.G. were about the same age. In March of YR-05, C.W. and M.F. were solemnly joined together in a commitment ceremony at All Saints Episcopal

Church in Bristol.

14. From the year YR-06 until the present, C.W. and M.F. have acted as co-parents of K.G. They share the joys and responsibilities of parenting, and K.G. considers them both to be her parents.

15. In April YR-04, C.W. was diagnosed with multiple sclerosis, a disabling and usually fatal disease of the brain and nervous system.

16. Because they wanted to formalize their status as a family, and to enable M.F. to discharge all the responsibilities and enjoy all the rights of a parent, and in recognition of C.W.'s increasing disability, M.F. and C.W. decided that M.F. should adopt K.G. M.F. filed an adoption petition on August 13, YR-01, in the defendant Chancery Court for Van Buren County, Mississippi, of which the defendant Rhodes is the Chancellor.

17. On August 22, YR-01, as permitted by Miss. Code Ann. § 93-17-11, the Chancellor referred M.F.'s petition to the Mississippi Department of Human Services (hereinafter "the Department") for an investigation and home study. Over the course of the next six months, a qualified and licensed social worker attached to the Department's Division of Children and Family Services conducted a thorough investigation of M.F., C.W., and K.G., and of their home, their backgrounds, and personal characteristics.

18. The Department's report, issued on March 1, YR-00, found that a decree granting M.F.'s petition to adopt K.G. would be in K.G.'s best interest. The report gave detailed and concrete reasons for that finding.

19. Nevertheless, M.F.'s desire to adopt K.G. and K.G.'s best interest were pushed aside by the Attorney General of Mississippi (the defendant Fender), the Mississippi Department of Human Services (directed by the defendant Ellison), and Chancery Court

of Van Buren County (per the defendant Rhodes), on the basis of a homophobic piece of legislation passed by the Mississippi legislature in the year 2000, Miss. Code § 93-17-3(5).

20. The bill that became Miss. Code § 93-17-3(5) was not enacted out of any concern for the welfare of children. Rather, it was enacted as a preemptive strike against same sex marriage. The legislature believed that if they denied same-gender couples the right to adopt and raise children, they could prevent courts from finding a basis upon which the benefits of marriage would be conferred upon such families.

21. In addition to complying with the unconstitutional prohibition of Miss. Code § 93-17-3(5), Chancellor Rhodes also purported to find that the adoption of K.G. by M.F. would not be in K.G.'s best interest. That purported finding was based on several subsidiary findings that have no support in the record before the Chancellor and are based on the Chancellor's subjective speculations. For example, in his memorandum opinion explaining the denial of M.F.'s petition, the Chancellor stated —

(A) "The interests of a child are rarely served by being adopted by a homosexual couple. The outcomes of homosexual adoptions are generally less successful for the children than the outcomes of adoptions by heterosexual couples." That statement not only is unsupported by the record before the Chancellor but is, in fact, false.

(B) "[T]he petitioner is emotionally dependent upon the older role models who have influenced her, and it is to them that she owes the fact that she has managed to keep up the appearance of stability in her life." The record before the Chancellor contained no evidence about the "appearance of stability" of M.F.'s life beyond her having escaped as a teenager from a chaotic life, having pulled herself up by the

bootstraps to graduate from high school, having graduated from college, having

established a successful career as an artist, and earning enough money on a regular

basis to support herself and her child. In fact, M.F.'s life is very stable and there are

no grounds for believing that will change.

(C)   "Petitioner's sole income is from her earnings as an artist. Artists' incomes

are notoriously unstable." The record before the Chancellor contained no evidence

about the stability of artists' incomes in general, or about whether M.F.'s financial

success is typical or atypical of artists generally. Furthermore, M.F.'s financial

stability is irrelevant to K.G.'s best interest because K.G. is independently supported

by a trust fund that is more than adequate to meet her needs. The Chancellor

disparaged this evidence by observing that "[p]etitioner's financial situation would be

greatly improved if she could gain control over K.G.'s trust fund." Yet

uncontroverted evidence in the record establishes that there is no way for M.F. to gain

control over the trust fund.

Claims for Relief

Count I: Substantive Due Process

22. Paragraphs 1-20 are incorporated by reference herein.

23. M.F. and C.W. each have constitutionally protected liberty and privacy interests

in creating families and family structures that will enable them and their children to

pursue their dreams, choose their lifestyles, and realize their full human potential.

24. K.G. has constitutionally protected liberty and privacy interests in being brought

up by parents who love and care for her and provide for her needs.

25. Mississippi Code § 93-17-3(5) deprives M.F., C.W., and K.G. of those interests without serving any countervailing state interest, and thus denies M.F., C.W., and K.G. due process of law.

Count II: Equal Protection

26. Counts 1-20 are incorporated by reference in herein.

27. M.F. and C.W.'s right to create a family of their own choosing, including the right to decide whether and under what circumstances to bring children into their lives, is a fundamental right that encompasses both biological and adoptive children. K.G.'s right to have her family's choices for her welfare be unimpeded by state interference is also a fundamental right. Mississippi Code § 93-17-3(5) deprives M.F., C.W., and K.G. of the aforementioned fundamental rights by discriminating between M.F., C.W., and K.G., on one hand, and other persons on the other hand. In doing so, it serves no compelling state interest and fails to utilize the least intrusive means of attempting to serve that interest.

28. In the alternative to an alternative to paragraph 27. The interests of M.F., C.W., and K.G., as described in paragraph 27, while perhaps not fundamental rights, are interests that deserve the law's solicitous protection and cannot be denied discriminatorily in the absence of a rational basis for the discrimination. There is no rational basis for the discrimination between same-gender couples and all other persons made by Miss. Code § 93-17-3(5).

Count III: Mississippi Law

29. Counts 1-19 and 21 are incorporated by reference herein.

30. Under Mississippi law, a judicial finding of fact cannot stand if it is utterly lacking in evidentiary support in the record before the tribunal or if it is based on

speculation. Accordingly, Mississippi law requires that the defendant Chancellor

Rhodes's determination in this case be set aside.

<u>Damages</u>

31. As a result of the defendants' unconstitutional actions, the integrity of the

plaintiffs' family has been damaged, the plaintiffs' reputation in their community has

been diminished, and the plaintiffs have suffered mental and emotional anguish and

distress.

<u>Equities</u>

32. The harms inflicted upon the plaintiffs as a result of the defendants'

unconstitutional actions are ongoing. Plaintiffs' have no adequate remedy at law to put an

end to those ongoing harms. While plaintiff's past damages are to a limited extent

compensable, for the most part they are irreparable. The plaintiffs come before the court

with clean hands.

WHEREFORE, plaintiffs pray for a judgment:

(A) Declaring that Miss. Code § 93-17-3(5) unconstitutionally deprives the plaintiffs

of liberty without due process of law;

(B) Declaring that Miss. Code § 93-17-3(5) deprives the plaintiffs of the equal

protection of the laws;

(C) Declaring that the decision of the Chancery Court of Van Buren County,

Mississippi, by which M.F. was not allowed to adopt K.G., is invalid and must be set

aside;

(D) Enjoining the Chancery Court to set aside that decision and to conduct further

proceedings in accordance with the judgment of this court;

(E) Enjoining the defendants Fender and Ellison to cease and desist from enforcing Miss. Code § 93-17-3(5);

(F) Awarding to the plaintiffs such amount of monetary damages as will compensate them for their losses resulting from the defendants' unconstitutional actions towards them;

(G) Awarding to the plaintiffs their costs of suit and reasonable attorneys' fees for prosecuting this action.

(H) Granting to the plaintiffs such other and further relief as this court deems just.

Each of us declares under penalty of perjury that the statements made in the foregoing complaint are, to the best of her knowledge, true.

[Plaintiffs' signatures submitted under seal.]

Dated: July 24, YR-00   Respectfully submitted,

Natalie Moldonado
_____
Natalie Moldonado
485 Court Street
Lofborough, MS 38706
Telephone: (756) 922-3828
Attorney for the plaintiffs M.F., C.W. & K.G.

[Summons and Return of Service Omitted]

M.F., et al.   )

                              Plaintiffs   )

)

vs.   )

)

CHANCERY COURT OF VAN   )

BUREN COUNTY, MISSISSIPPI, et al.,   )

)

                              Defendants   )

UNITED STATES DISTRICT COURT
FILED
August 1, YR-00
MIDDLE DISTRICT OF MISSISSIPPI

Civil Action No. YR-00-3975

MOTION TO DISMISS COUNT III OF THE COMPLAINT
FOR LACK OF SUBJECT MATTER JURISDICTION

The defendants hereby move to dismiss Count III of the complaint pursuant to Fed. R. Civ. P. 12(b)(1) on the grounds that this court, in the exercise of its discretion under 28 U.S.C. § 1367(c), should decline to exercise supplemental jurisdiction over that count.

The complaint attacks a state court ruling denying M.F.'s petition to adopt K.G. Counts I and II attack that ruling on federal constitutional grounds, while Count III attacks it on state law grounds. Plaintiffs' only basis for claiming subject matter jurisdiction over Count III is supplemental jurisdiction pursuant to 28 U.S.C. § 1367. While all three counts seem to be part of a single case or controversy, and therefore qualify for the first step under § 1367(a), the court should nonetheless decline to exercise supplemental jurisdiction because of factors set forth in § 1367(c) should preclude the court from taking the second step by making a discretionary determination that the court should exercise supplemental jurisdiction. Three of those factors are relevant here:

(1) Count III raises a novel issue of State law. Unlike disputes involving child custody, there are no Mississippi court decisions indicating how sexual orientation should be weighed in determining the best interests of the child in the setting of an uncontested petition for adoption. Custody and adoption are sufficiently distinctive that the issue under Count III is not necessarily governed by prior decisions about custody. The issue under Count III is truly unprecedented in Mississippi.

(2) Count III substantially predominates over claims in Counts I and II, over which the district court has original jurisdiction, and (3) there are other compelling reasons for declining jurisdiction. Generally speaking, an issue as to the constitutionality of a state statute should not be addressed if that issue can be

avoided by a ruling on the construction or application of the statute. Count III raises an issue solely of state law, which the courts of Mississippi are peculiarly competent to address. Count III should be dismissed to give plaintiffs an opportunity to raise that claim in a Mississippi court.

Dated: August 1, YR-00

Respectfully submitted,

Gavin Peter Hess

Gavin Peter Hess
Deputy Attorney General of Mississippi

Attorney for the defendants, Chancery Court of Van Buren County, Mississippi; Lucas Rhodes, Chancellor of the Chancery Court for Van Buren County, Mississippi; Cody Ellison, Director of the Mississippi Department of Human Services; and Tommy Fender, Attorney General of the State of Mississippi.

Mississippi Attorney General's Office
State Justice Building
450 Broad Street
Jackson, MS 39201
Telephone: 601-459-4680

CERTIFICATE OF SERVICE

I certify that on this 1st day of August, YR-00, I served the attached Motion to Dismiss Count III of the Complaint For Lack of Subject Matter Jurisdiction upon the plaintiffs by causing a copy thereof to be mailed, first class postage prepaid, to the attorney for the plaintiffs, Natalie Moldonado, Esquire, 485 Court Street, Lofborough, MS 38706.

Gavin Peter Hess

Gavin Peter Hess
Deputy Attorney General of Mississippi
Mississippi Attorney General's Office
State Justice Building
450 Broad Street
Jackson, MS 39201
Telephone: 601-459-4680

M.F., et al.
 	
                              Plaintiffs
 	
          vs.
 	
CHANCERY COURT OF VAN
BUREN COUNTY, MISSISSIPPI, et al.,
 	
                              Defendants
	)
	)
	)
	)
	)
	)
	)
	)
	)
	)

UNITED STATES DISTRICT
COURT
FILED
𝒮𝑒𝓅𝓉𝑒𝓂𝒷𝑒𝓇 2, 𝒴ℛ-00
MIDDLE DISTRICT OF MISSISSIPPI

Civil Action No. YR-00-3975

MOTION TO DISMISS COUNTS I and II OF THE COMPLAINT
FOR FAILURE TO STATE A CLAIM

The defendants hereby move pursuant to Fed. R. Civ. P. 12(b)(6) to dismiss Counts I and II of the Complaint because both fail to state a claim upon which relief can be granted.

Counts I and II of the complaint allege that Mississippi Code § 93-17-3(5) denies plaintiffs substantive due process and equal protection of the law in violation of the Fourteenth Amendment to the U.S. Constitution. As a matter of law, however, the statute does not impair any fundamental right held by plaintiffs and it does not discriminate against a federally protected class of individuals. The statute's prohibition on adoption by couples of the same gender does rationally and reasonably further legitimate government interests. Because a rational relationship to a legitimate government interest is all that is required to uphold the law, Counts I and II should be dismissed.

Dated: September 2, YR-00   Respectfully submitted,

                                             Gavin Peter Hess
                                             Gavin Peter Hess
                                             Deputy Attorney General of Mississippi

                                             Attorney for the defendants, Chancery
                                             Court of Van Buren County, Mississippi;
                                             Lucas Rhodes, Chancellor of the Chancery
                                             Court for Van Buren County, Mississippi;
                                             Cody Ellison, Director of the Mississippi

Department of Human Services; and
Tommy Fender, Attorney General of the
State of Mississippi.

Mississippi Attorney General's Office
State Justice Building
450 Broad Street
Jackson, MS 39201
Telephone: 601-459-4680

CERTIFICATE OF SERVICE

I certify that on this 2nd day of September, YR-00, I served the attached Motion to Dismiss Counts I and II of the Complaint For Failure to State a Claim upon the plaintiffs by causing a copy thereof to be mailed, first class postage prepaid, to the attorney for the plaintiffs, Natalie Moldonado, Esquire, 485 Court Street, Lofborough, MS 38706.

Gavin Peter Hess

Gavin Peter Hess
Deputy Attorney General of Mississippi
Mississippi Attorney General's Office
State Justice Building
450 Broad Street
Jackson, MS 39201
Telephone: 601-459-4680

Gavin Peter Hess
Deputy Attorney General, State of Mississippi
State Justice Building
450 Broad Street
Jackson, MS 39201
Telephone: 601-459-4680

Attorney for Defendants
Chancery Court of Van Buren County, Mississippi
Lucas Rhodes, Chancellor of the Van Buren County
Chancery Court
Cody Ellison, Director, Mississippi Dept. of Human Services
Tommy Fender, Attorney General, State of Mississippi

In the

United States District Court
for the Middle District of Mississippi

M.F., et al.	)	UNITED STATES DISTRICT COURT
	)	FILED
Plaintiffs	)	*October 3, YR -00*
	)	MIDDLE DISTRICT OF MISSISSIPPI
vs.	)	
	)	
CHANCERY COURT OF VAN	)	
BUREN COUNTY, MISSISSIPPI, et al.,	)	
	)	Civil Action No. YR-00-
3975		
Defendants	)	

DEFENDANTS' ANSWER TO THE COMPLAINT

This answer is filed on behalf of defendants Chancery Court of Van Buren County,

Mississippi; Lucas Rhodes, Chancellor of the Van Buren County Chancery Court; Cody

Ellison, Director of the Mississippi Department of Human Services; and Tommy Fender,

Attorney General of the State of Mississippi. They are hereinafter referred to collectively as "Defendants."

1. Defendants admit the first sentence of paragraph 1 of the Complaint. They deny the remainder of paragraph 1.

2. Defendants are without knowledge or information sufficient to form a belief as to the truth of paragraph 3.

3. Defendants admit the first two sentences of paragraph 3, but deny the remainder of paragraph 3.

4. Defendants are without knowledge or information sufficient to form a belief as to the truth of paragraph 4.

5-8. Defendants admit paragraphs 5 through 8 of the Complaint with the assumption that paragraph 7 is intended to refer to Miss. Code Ann. § 93-17-3(5).

9-16. Defendants are without knowledge or information sufficient to form a belief as to the truth of paragraphs 9 through 16 of the Complaint.

17. Defendants admit paragraph 17.

18-33. Defendants deny paragraphs 18 through 21, 27 through 29, and 31 through 33 of the Complaint. Paragraphs 22, 26, and 30 of the Complaint each incorporate by reference paragraphs 1 through 21 of the Complaint. In response to paragraphs 22, 26, and 30, defendants incorporate their responses to paragraphs 1 through 21.

First Affirmative Defense

34.   Counts I, II, and III of the Complaint each fail to state a claim upon which relief should be granted.

Second Affirmative Defense

35.   The court lacks subject matter jurisdiction over Count III of the Complaint.

Dated: October 3, YR-00

Respectfully submitted,

Gavin Peter Hess

Gavin Peter Hess
Deputy Attorney General of
Mississippi
Attorney for the defendants,
Chancery Court of Van Buren
County, Mississippi;
Lucas Rhodes, Chancellor of
the Chancery Court for Van
Buren County, Mississippi;
Cody Ellison, Director of the
Mississippi Department of
Human Services; and
Tommy Fender, Attorney
General of the State of
Mississippi.

Mississippi Attorney General's
Office
State Justice Building
450 Broad Street
Jackson, MS 39201
Telephone: 601-459-4680

<u>CERTIFICATE OF SERVICE</u>

I certify that on this 3rd day of October, YR-00, I served the attached Defendants'

Answer upon the plaintiffs by causing a copy thereof to be mailed, first class postage

prepaid, to the attorney for the plaintiffs, Natalie Moldonado, Esquire, 485 Court Street,

Lofborough, MS 38706.

Gavin Peter Hess
_____
Gavin Peter Hess
Deputy Attorney General of Mississippi
Mississippi Attorney General's Office
State Justice Building
450 Broad Street
Jackson, MS 39201
Telephone: 601-459-4680

Gavin Peter Hess
Deputy Attorney General, State of Mississippi
State Justice Building
450 Broad Street
Jackson, MS 39201
Telephone: 601-459-4680

Attorney for Defendants
Chancery Court of Van Buren County, Mississippi
Lucas Rhodes, Chancellor of the Van Buren County Chancery Court
Cody Ellison, Director, Mississippi Dept. of Human Services
Tommy Fender, Attorney General, State of Mississippi

In the
United States District Court
for the Middle District of Mississippi

M.F., et al.	)	UNITED STATES DISTRICT COURT
	)	FILED
Plaintiffs	)	*October* 14, *YR*-00
	)	MIDDLE DISTRICT OF
vs.	)	MISSISSIPPI
	)	
CHANCERY COURT OF VAN	)	
BUREN COUNTY, MISSISSIPPI, et al.,	)	
	)	Civil Action No. YR-00-3975
Defendants	)	

DEFENDANTS' MOTION FOR SUMMARY JUDGMENT
ON COUNTS I, II, AND III OF THE COMPLAINT

The defendants hereby move pursuant to Federal Rule of Civil Procedure 56 for

summary judgment on Counts I, II, and III of the Complaint. This motion is based on the

declaration of Arvid K. Tolak, Ph.D., which is filed herewith, and the memorandum of

points and authorities in support of this motion that will be filed with the Court no later than October 31, YR-00.

Count I of the Complaint alleges that Mississippi Code § 93-17-3(5) denies

plaintiffs substantive due process in violation of the Fourteenth Amendment to the U.S.

Constitution. Based on the undisputed facts, that statute does not impair any fundamental

right of plaintiffs, and its prohibition on adoption by couples of the same gender rationally

and reasonably furthers legitimate government interests. Defendants are, therefore,

entitled to judgment as a matter of law on Count I.

Count II of the Complaint alleges that Mississippi Code § 93-17-3(5) denies

plaintiffs equal protection of the law in violation of the Fourteenth Amendment to the

U.S. Constitution. Based on the undisputed facts, that statute does not discriminate

against any federally protected class of individuals and does not treat similarly situated

people differently. The prohibition on adoption by couples of the same gender rationally

and reasonably furthers legitimate government interests. Defendants are, therefore,

entitled to judgment as a matter of law on Count II.

Count III of the Complaint alleges a claim under Mississippi law, and this Court

has asserted supplemental jurisdiction over that claim. Because the Eleventh Amendment

bars a state law claim brought against state officials in federal district court even if the

court would otherwise have supplemental jurisdiction over that claim, defendants are

entitled to judgment as a matter of law on Count III.   Defendants have not waived their right to sovereign immunity under the Eleventh Amendment.

Dated: October 14, YR-00   Respectfully submitted,

                                             Gavin Peter Hess

                                             Gavin Peter Hess
                                             Deputy Attorney General
                                             of Mississippi

                                             Attorney for the defendants

                                             Mississippi Attorney
                                             General's Office
                                             State Justice Building

450 Broad Street

                                             Jackson, MS 39201
                                             Telephone: 601-459-4680

CERTIFICATE OF SERVICE

I certify that on this 14th day of October, YR-00, I served the attached Motion for Summary Judgment upon the plaintiffs by causing a copy thereof to be mailed, first class postage prepaid, to the attorney for the plaintiffs, Natalie Moldonado, Esquire, 485 Court Street, Lofborough, MS 38706.

Gavin Peter Hess
_____
Gavin Peter Hess
Deputy Attorney General of Mississippi
Mississippi Attorney General's Office
State Justice Building
450 Broad Street
Jackson, MS 39201
Telephone: 601-459-4680

In the
United States District Court
for the Middle District of Mississippi

M.F., et al.   )
)
                        Plaintiffs   )   Civil Action No. YR-00-3975
)
                        vs.   )   ┌─────────────────────────┐
)   │ UNITED STATES DISTRICT │
)   │   COURT   │
CHANCERY COURT OF VAN   )   │   FILED   │
BUREN COUNTY, MISSISSIPPI, et al.,   )   │   │
)   │   October 14, YR-00   │
                        Defendants   )   │   MIDDLE DISTRICT OF   │
                                                         │   MISSISSIPPI   │
                                                         └─────────────────────────┘

DECLARATION OF ARVID K. TOLAK, Ph.D.

I, Arvid K. Tolak, Ph.D., hereby declare as follows:

1. I am a professor of Social Psychology at Western Mississippi State University in Broadmoor, Mississippi. I received my undergraduate education at the University of Mississippi in Oxford, Mississippi. I pursued graduate studies in sociology and psychology at Yale University in New Haven, Connecticut, and at the University of Florida in Gainesville, Florida. I was awarded a Ph.D. degree in social psychology in 1985 by the University of Florida. I joined the faculty of Western Mississippi State University in 1983 as a lecturer. I was appointed to the rank of assistant professor in the psychology department in 1985, was granted tenure and promoted to the rank of associate professor in 1990, and was promoted to full professor in 1993. In the 1999-2000 academic year, I served as the acting chair of the Department of Psychology. I am a member in good standing of both the American and the Mississippi Psychological Associations. I have published three books and more than three dozen articles in my fields

of particular interest, which include discrimination against persons with mental illness, social structures for treating mental illness, and social science research methodology. I have testified in court on seven occasions and have qualified as an expert in the fields of research psychology and sociology.

2. I am writing this declaration at the request of the attorneys for the defendants in this litigation in order to provide information and expert testimony as to the bases underlying Mississippi's legislative prohibition of adoption by couples of the same sex, Mississippi Code § 93-17-3(5). I was a resident of Mississippi before, during, and after the political campaign that led to the adoption of that legislation. I am familiar with the newspaper coverage of that legislation, and I have conversed extensively with its political supporters and opponents. I am professionally very familiar with the social science literature on homosexuality, especially as it relates to such issues as homosexual marriage and the adoption of children by homosexuals. I am also very familiar with legislation affecting the legal status of homosexuals.

3.   Mississippi law has not been hospitable to claims of discrimination based on sexual orientation. Mississippi statutes barring various forms of discrimination in state services and state funded services have been enacted since about 20 years ago; these statutes commonly outlaw discrimination on such bases as race, color, religion, national origin, and handicap, but consistently fail to include sexual orientation. See, in chronological order of enactment: Miss. Code §§ 25-9-149 (added 1984) (state employment), 57-61-19 (added 1986) (business investment act), 57-71-19 (added 1988) (small enterprise development financing), 43-33-723 (added 1989) (low income housing), 93-21-107(3) (added 1990) (domestic violence shelters), 57-10-519 (added 1993) (small business assistance), 41-95-7 (added 1994) (health finance authority), 57-77-27 (added 1994) (venture capital act); see Code of Judicial Conduct, Canon 2A (added 2002) (forbidding judges belonging to organizations that practice "invidious discrimination on

the basis of race, gender, religion or national origin"); *cf.* Miss. Code § 99-19-301, -307 (added 1994) (penalty enhancement for felonies committed for discriminatory reasons). In connection with "sex-related education," as to which "abstinence education" is the "state standard," children must be taught "the current state law related to sexual conduct, including forcible rape, statutory rape, paternity establishment, child support and homosexual activity." Miss. Code § 37-13-171 (added 1998). Only two exceptions to this pattern of non-inclusion of sexual orientation appear in Mississippi statutory law. They are both of recent origin: Code of Judicial Conduct, Canon 3B(5) (added 2002) ("A judge shall not, in the performance of judicial duties, by words or conduct manifest bias or prejudice, including but not limited to bias or prejudice based upon race, gender, religion, national origin, disability, age, *sexual orientation* or socioeconomic status, and shall not permit staff, court officials and others subject to the judge's direction and control to do so.") (emphasis added); and a provision of the Health Care Conscience Act, which allows a health care provider to refuse to participate in a health care service that violates his or her conscience, but also states that the refusal cannot be based on "the patient's race, color, national origin, ethnicity, sex, religion, creed or *sexual orientation*." Miss. Code § 41-107-5 (added 2004) (emphasis added).

    4.   Mississippi has enacted two major pieces of legislation regarding family relationships of homosexuals. Both of them were in immediate response to legal developments in other jurisdictions. The bases of these statutes can be discerned to some extent from their plain language and to some extent from their history. In addition, there are available contemporaneous statements to journalists by members of the legislature, which are quoted herein as evidence of what the legislators had in mind and not as a substitute for legislative debates and committee reports, which Mississippi does not maintain. *Steadman v. Mississippi Farm Bur. Cas. Ins. Co.*, 626 So.2d 588, 591 (Miss. 1993).

5. The first major piece of legislation was triggered by the decision of a circuit court in Hawaii, which held that Hawaii's refusal to grant marriage licenses to homosexual couples violated the state's constitutional guarantee of equal protection of the laws. *Baehr v. Miike*, Civil No. 91-1394, 1996 WL 694235 (Haw. Cir. Ct. Dec. 3, 1996). Two years later, the legislature and voters of Hawaii overturned that ruling by adopting a constitutional amendment granting the legislature power to reserve marriage to opposite sex couples. *See Baehr v. Miike*, No. 20371, 1999 Haw. LEXIS 391 (Haw. 1999). In the interim, however, the Hawaii circuit court's decision had prompted the legislatures of many states to consider the status of same-sex marriages.

6. On February 12, 1997, Mississippi enacted legislation providing that: "Any marriage between persons of the same gender is prohibited and null and void from the beginning. Any marriage between persons of the same gender that is valid in another jurisdiction does not constitute a legal or valid marriage in Mississippi." Miss. Code § 93-1-1(2) (added 1997). A similar provision was inserted in the Mississippi Constitution in 2004. Miss. Const. Art. 14 § 263A.

7. The official attitude towards homosexual marriages in Mississippi is captured in the following report of statements by Governor Fordice when he signed the 1997 bill:

> "For too long in this freedom-loving land, cultural subversives have engaged in trench warfare on traditional family values," Fordice said during a bill signing ceremony in his Capitol office. ¶ "These radical subgroups have distorted the national agenda and defiled time-honored customs for their own selfish purposes," he said. ¶ The governor also said the state should ensure gay couples do not enjoy benefits of marriage such as health insurance. ¶ "Insurance benefits for dependents were never intended for perverse relationships such as the same-sex marriage," he said. "They were intended for traditional families." * * * ¶ Fordice, a Republican who has enjoyed widespread support among religious groups in the state, talked Wednesday about the importance of marriage. ¶ "Through the history of

civilization, marriage has been a contract between a single man and a single woman," he said. "Therein is based the family, which is the glue that has held civilization together for all these thousands of years. When that glue begins to break down, families begin to break down." Mississippi is the latest state to respond to a gay rights case in Hawaii. A judge there has ruled that Hawaii must grant marriage licenses to gay couples, though the decision is being appealed. ¶ "The whole nation has felt threatened by the actions in Hawaii," Fordice said.

Gina Holland, *Fordice Bans Gay Marriage, ACLU Says Law Is Intolerant*, The Sun Herald (Biloxi, MS), Feb. 13, 1997, at A1.

8.   Three years later, on December 20, 1999, the Vermont Supreme Court held that the common benefits clause of the Vermont constitution compelled that state's legislature to extend the benefits of marriage to same sex couples. *Baker v. State*, 744 A.2d 864 (1999). This was the first such holding by the highest court of a state. The court stated that one of the principal advantages of civil marriage is to promote security for children. The court noted that significant numbers of heterosexual couples elect to be childless, while significant numbers of same-sex couples are raising children acquired through either adoption or alternative methods of child bearing, such as artificial insemination and surrogacy. Because of its disparate treatment of the children of same-sex and opposite-sex couples, the court held that the restriction of marriage to opposite-sex couples was both underinclusive and overinclusive in its promotion of the state's interest in the welfare of children. The Vermont decision, with its linkage of a constitutional right of homosexuals to enjoy the benefits of marriage with a right of homosexuals to raise children, was widely publicized throughout the United States, including Mississippi. Policy makers in several states began debating the issue of same sex adoptions, "fueled by recognition of gay unions in Vermont." Gina Holland, *State Bans Adoption by Gay Couples – ACLU: Decision Likely to Bring Lawsuits*, The Sun Herald (Biloxi, MS), Apr. 20, 2000 at A4.

9.   On January 12, 2000, the first day for introducing bills in the 2000 Regular Session of the Mississippi Legislature, Representative Bobby B. Howell introduced House Bill No. 49, to amend Section 93-17-3 of the Mississippi Code of 1972 by adding at the end thereof a new subsection (2), reading as follows: "Adoption by couples of the same gender is prohibited. Any adoption by couples of the same gender that is valid in another jurisdiction does not constitute a legal or valid adoption in Mississippi." The bill was referred to Judiciary Committee A. (See H.B. 49 at <http://billstatus.ls.state.ms.us/ 2000/html/daily_action/011200.htm>.) A subcommittee held a hearing on the bill, and the Committee reported it out to the House with a recommendation that it "do pass."

10.   On the day of the deadline for bringing House Bill No. 49 to a floor vote in the House, the Chairman of the House Judiciary Committee A skipped over it on the calendar (as was his prerogative), and the bill therefore died. Emily Wagster, *Bill to Ban Adoption by Gay Couples Dies*, The Clarion-Ledger (Jackson, MS), Mar. 17, 2000, at 5B.

11.   Supporters of the bill were outraged. They organized a "telephone blitz" that was so successful that the House switchboard was jammed. However, the time for introducing new bills had passed. The House Public Health and Welfare Committee revived the issue by adding part of the language of House Bill No. 49 to a pre-existing bill authorizing nurse practitioners to sign certificates dealing with the health of a child being considered for adoption. (House Bill No. 3074.) Joseph Ammerman, *Bill Barring Gay Adoption Revived in House*, The Clarion-Ledger (Jackson, MS), Mar. 22, 2000, at 1A.

12.   The language added to House Bill No. 3074 did not include the provision of House Bill No. 49 that purported to invalidate adoptions by same-sex couples granted in other states. A chief opponent of adoptions by same-sex couples expressed his disappointment at this omission, saying, "[f]orcing us to recognize adoptions done out of state would be the same thing as forcing us to recognize marriage of homosexuals in other

states. ... [Those states do not] have the same moral values of what we have in Mississippi." A legislator defended the omission on the ground that the state could be successfully sued over a law failing to recognize adoptions in other states. Gina Holland, *House Resurrects Bill to Ban Gay Adoption,* The Sun Herald (Biloxi, MS), Mar. 22, 2000, at A6. House Bill No. 3074 was passed by overwhelming majorities in both the House and the Senate, and was signed by the Governor on May 3, 2000.

13.   Statements by supporters of the bill, both inside and outside the legislature, indicate that the primary basis for it was to preserve traditional family values.

A.   "There is no way you can convince me that 'Joe has two mommies' is a value we need to extend to the next generation." Statement of Rep. Rita Martinson, member of House Judiciary Subcommittee, in Emily Wagster, *Bill to Ban Adoptions by Same-Sex Couples Advances,* The Clarion-Ledger (Jackson MS), Feb. 23, 2000, at 5B.

B.   "Lawmakers ought to make sure that we not sentence a child who has already had one bad turn in life to something we know is improper and immoral." Rep. Gary Chism, R-Columbus. Rep. Gary Chism, in Gina Holland, *Gay Couple Adoption Ban Passed*, Mar. 8, 2000, at <http://www.gfn.com/archives/ story. phtml?sid=5176>.

C.   "Forcing us to recognize adoptions done out of state would be the same thing as forcing us to recognize marriage of homosexuals in other states... [Those states do not] have the same moral values of what we have in Mississippi." Mike Crook, state director of American Family Association, in Gina Holland, *House Resurrects Bill to Ban Gay Adoptions*, The Sun Herald (Biloxi, MS), Mar. 22, 2000, at A6.

D.   "I just think a traditional family atmosphere is the best way to raise a child." Rep. Bobby Howell, in Joseph Ammerman, *Legislation Barring Gay Couples From Adopting Children – Thought to Be Dead Last Week – Could Come Up For Action in the House as Early as Today*, The Clarion-Ledger (Jackson, MS), Mar. 22, 2000, at 1A.

E.   "What constitutes a family is not a homosexual couple." Rep. Bobby Moody, Chairman, House Public Health Committee, in Gina Holland, *Miss. House OK's Bill Banning Gay Adoptions*, Memphis Commercial Appeal (TN), Mar. 23, 2000, at A10.

F.   "We are grateful to God that they have passed it, and we would stand behind them and urge them to continue to stand for the traditional values of family, home and Christian values that Mississippi has enjoyed through these years." Rev. Kermit D. McGregor, president of the Mississippi Baptist Convention, in Emily Wagster & Joseph Ammerman, *Ban on Gay Adoption Headed to Musgrove*, The Clarion-Ledger (Jackson MS), Apr. 20, 2000, at 1B.

G.   Most senators said the proposal bolsters family values. Gina Holland, *State Bans Adoption by Gay Couples – ACLU: Decision Likely to Bring Lawsuits*, The Sun Herald (Biloxi, MS), Apr. 20, 2000 at A4.

H.   The new law represents "the traditional values of home, family and Christian values that most Mississippians agree upon." Rev. Kermit D. McGregor (see D, above), in Emily Wagster, *Adoption Ban Targeting Gays Stirs Emotions*, The Clarion-Ledger (Jackson, MS), May 15, 2000, at 1B.

I.   "I think it sets a tone for our state. I mean, you want to get back to a lot of the moral issues. And I know that it's tough to legislate morality, but when you look at adoptions, you want a child to go into a house with a father and a mother, in a traditional home setting." Sen. Tim Johnson, in *id.*

J.   "I don't see how you can teach morality when what you're practicing is immoral. It's a dangerous place for a child to be put into." Mike Crook, state director of American Family Association, in Gina Holland, *Parenting Hopes Put on Hold; Law Says Gays Can't Adopt,* The Sun Herald (Biloxi, MS), July 9, 2000, at A12.

K.   "Homosexuals have already made a mistake, as long as they're on that road it's going to be hard to be good parents. While a gay couple may be able to provide housing, food, and things that money can buy for a child, they can't do the job of raising a child the right way." Sen Richard White, in *id.*

14.   Supporters and opponents alike acknowledged that the bill was not addressed to an existing problem but was, rather, <u>a preemptive move against a perceived homosexual agenda.</u>

A.   "It was a preventative measure. Chancery judges have so much authority in Mississippi that it's possible that one would grant an adoption to a gay couple. I think most people in Mississippi recognize that would not be healthy for a child." Forest Thigpen, Mississippi Family Council President, in Emily Wagster, *Bill to Ban Adoption by Gay Couples Dies*, The Clarion-Ledger (Jackson, MS), Mar. 17, 2000, at 5B.

B.   Even though many legislators privately admit chances of any gay couple adopting a child in Mississippi are poor now, when such adoptions have to be approved by a Chancery Judge, Crook says he's interested in passing a law that protects children in the future. "We feel like in many instances we've seen the homosexuals move forward in the courts to force their agenda upon us. We don't want to leave it in the hands of a few people to make decisions about law here in Mississippi." Mike Crook, state director of American Family Association, in Joseph Ammerman, *Legislation Barring Gay Couples From Adopting Children – Thought to Be Dead Last Week – Could Come Up For Action in the House as Early as Today*, The Clarion-Ledger (Jackson, MS), Mar. 22, 2000, at 1A.

C.   The bill was prompted by public pressure from religious groups instead of real cases of gay adoptive parents... Bill opponents and supporters said they were unaware of adoptions in Mississippi involving gay couples. Gina Holland, *Miss. House OK's Bill Banning Gay Adoptions*, Memphis Commercial Appeal (TN), Mar. 23, 2000, at A10.

D.   See also Emily Wagster, *Bill to Ban Adoptions by Same-Sex Couples Advances,* The Clarion-Ledger (Jackson MS), Feb. 23, 2000, at 5B; Emily Wagster, *Adoption Ban Targeting Gays Stirs Emotions*, The Clarion-Ledger (Jackson, MS), May 15, 2000, at 1B.

15. Several supporters of the bill referred to <u>future harms</u> that they anticipated children adopted by homosexuals would suffer, such as —

A.   <u>Becoming homosexual</u> themselves.

i. Studies show that children of gay parents are more likely to be gay than children of straight parents. These children will be influenced in a way we don't want them to be influenced." Statement of Rev. Jim Futral, executive director of Mississippi Baptist Convention Board, at hearing before House

Judiciary Subcommittee, in Emily Wagster, *Bill to Ban Adoptions by Same-Sex Couples Advances,* The Clarion-Ledger (Jackson MS), Feb. 23, 2000, at 5B.

ii. Many of the issue's supporters say children raised in gay families are at risk of abuse or having a gay lifestyle forced upon them. Joseph Ammerman, *Legislation Barring Gay Couples From Adopting Children – Thought to Be Dead Last Week – Could Come Up For Action in the House as Early as Today*, The Clarion-Ledger (Jackson, MS), Mar. 22, 2000, at 1A.

iii. Mississippi has a responsibility to protect children. Crook said his primary fears are gender identity problems for the child and possible sexual abuse. "I don't see how you can teach morality when what you're practicing is immoral. It's a dangerous place for a child to be put into. They have trouble determining what they should be." Mike Crook, state director of American Family Association, in Gina Holland, *Parenting Hopes Put on Hold; Law Says Gays Can't Adopt,* The Sun Herald (Biloxi, MS, July 9, 2000, at A12.

B. <u>Being abused</u>. See A. ii., iii, above; "That bill is of the assumption that anybody who's gay will abuse children." Rep. David Green (an opponent) in Gina Holland, *Miss. House OK's Bill Banning Gay Adoptions*, Memphis Commercial Appeal (TN), Mar. 23, 2000, at A10.

C. <u>Instability</u>. Adopted children should go to parents with stable relationships. I don't think same-sex couples would offer stability. Statement of Rep. Rita Martinson, member of House Judiciary Subcommittee, in Emily Wagster, *Bill to Ban Adoptions by Same-Sex Couples Advances,* The Clarion-Ledger (Jackson MS), Feb. 23, 2000, at 5B.

D. Imbalance. "Kids turn out more balanced having a traditional family – a mother and a father." Rep. Gary Chism, R-Columbus. Rep. Gary Chism, in Gina Holland, *Gay Couple Adoption Ban Passed*, Mar. 8, 2000, at <http://www.gfn.com/archives/story.phtml?sid=5176>.

E. Exposure to an unnatural lifestyle. "As legislators, we're charged with the responsibility of protecting children. We shouldn't place them in a lifestyle that's unnatural." Statement of Rep. Gary Chism, member of House Judiciary Subcommittee. Emily Wagster, *Bill to Ban Adoptions by Same-Sex Couples Advances,* The Clarion-Ledger (Jackson MS), Feb. 23, 2000, at 5B.

F. Exposure to illegal conduct. "Sodomy is a crime in Mississippi. A homosexual relationship implies the exercise of illegal activities, and no child should be permitted to enter that setting." Sen. Ron Farris, in Gina Holland, *State Bans Adoption by Gay Couples – ACLU: Decision Likely to Bring Lawsuits*, The Sun Herald (Biloxi, MS), Apr. 20, 2000 at A4.

16.   Social science does not address value judgments or political motivations. It does, however, have the potential to address issues of human behavior and predictions of probable outcomes of recurrent social situations. The most valuable scientific studies of the effects of recurrent social situations on human behavior are those that can be carried out over a long period time, so that both short range and long term effects can be observed; and those that use such techniques as probability sampling, random selection of subjects, control groups, double-blind techniques to counteract biases, and statistical analysis to distinguish between significant and insignificant correlations. Unfortunately from the viewpoint of science, the incidence of adoptions by homosexuals has been minuscule until recent times. Also, there is so much stigma attached to homosexuality in the United States that truly randomized selection of subjects is extremely difficult, if not

impossible. Nevertheless, an abundant literature about the effects of homosexual parenting in comparison to heterosexual parenting has begun to develop in the past decade.

17. At the present time there is controversy within the scientific literature as to the effect upon a child of being adopted and brought up by a couple of the same gender. I understand that it is not my responsibility to evaluate the relevant literature and resolve the controversy. Rather, I have been asked to call the court's attention to the those parts of the scientific literature that might be considered in determining whether the 2000 amendment to Miss. Code § 93-17-3 is a rationally based means of attaining legitimate

state interests.

18. The investigators whose research is most supportive of the probability of harm to children raised by homosexuals are Paul Cameron, Ph.D., and Kirk Cameron, Ph.D., of the Family Research Institute, Inc., of Colorado Springs, Colorado. Their classic study, *Homosexual Parents*, was published in the journal ADOLESCENCE, vol. 31, No. 124, pp. 757-776 (Winter 1996). The article was based on questionnaires obtained from 5,182 randomly obtained adults from six U.S. cities, of whom 17 indicated that they had a homosexual parent. The Camerons abstracted their conclusions as follows:

> Parental homosexuality may be related to findings that: (1) 5 of the 17 reported sexual relations with their parents; (2) a disproportionate fraction reported sexual relations with other caretakers and relatives; and (3) a disproportionate fraction (a) claimed a less than exclusively heterosexual orientation (47%); (b) indicated gender dissatisfaction; and (c) reported that their first sexual experience was homosexual. [*Id.* at 757.]

19. In their *Homosexual Parents* article, the authors also examined the research and writings of others in search of validation or refutation of the following "traditional opinions":

> [H]omosexual parents would tend to have the following effects upon their children: (1) provide a model, associates, and experiences that would make a child

more apt to engage in homosexuality and therefore become homosexual, (2) increase the probability of various forms of childhood sexual victimization (from parents and their associates), and (3) because the parents' worldview and behavioral standards are disturbed, the child would be more apt to be socially and psychologically disturbed than would children raise by nonhomosexual parents. [*Id.* at 768.]

The authors concluded that each of the "traditional opinions" had not been refuted, and in fact, (1) "whatever the mechanism, homosexual parents are associated disproportionately with homosexual children"; (2) there is a "disproportionate association between homosexuality and pedophilia," and therefore "a correspondingly disproportionate risk of homosexual incest ... for children reared by homosexuals," and (3) "[t]he limited evidence we assembled is consonant with the notion that children raised by homosexuals disproportionately experience divorce and that the circumstances of childhood may be disproportionately reported as emotionally harmful ..." *Id.* at 769, 771, 772.

20.   Another series of studies by the Cameron group employed a data base constructed from appellate court opinions in cases involving appeals of contested child custody decisions. See Paul Cameron & David W. Harris, *Homosexual Parents in Custody Disputes: A Thousand Child-Years Exposure*, 93 PSYCHOLOGICAL REPORTS 1173 (2003). Beginning with book research (the Decennial Digest and Shepards), which they supplemented with electronic research (Westlaw), the Camerons collected cases reporting 77 different disputes between a homosexual and a heterosexual parent; and also a group of 78 randomly selected control cases reporting disputes between exclusively heterosexual parents. The Camerons extolled the reliability of these data, as follows:

> The Appeals literature is a set of highly intrusive information regarding homosexual custody of children. The highest societal standards of evidence and proof are employed in such decisions. As the findings do not depend upon volunteers (as in the bulk of comparative or interview studies) and are not compromised in unknown ways by refusals (as always happen in random surveys), in veridical empirical content the Appeals literature stands head and shoulders above social science surveys or interviews of any kind. Its chief weakness lies in

not knowing how representative of homosexual parents in general such information might be. [*Id.* at 1176-1177; see also *id.* at 1187-1188.]

The reports of the cases were analyzed and coded according to whether any child involved in the dispute had been reported as fundamentally harmed or unharmed, and, if harmed, according to the nature of the harm. The recorded harms included hypersexualization or eroticization, subjected to pressure or evangelism to accept homosexuality, physically or sexually abused, teased, sexually confused, alienated by one parent from the other, subject to a false charge of molestation, unstabilized either mentally or residentially or by parental loss of employment, neglected, or emotionally disturbed. The apparent source of each harm was recorded. The reports were also coded for reported instances parental of lying or criminality by either parents or their associates. *Id.* at 1178-1179.

21.   The *Custody Disputes* study concluded that:

[H]omosexual parents in general exhibited poorer character [than nonhomosexual parents] as indexed by lying or criminality. They were also more apt to be recorded as having harmed children and more apt to be recorded as exposing them to harms. ... [T]he 142 children exposed to both a homosexual and a nonhomosexual parent suffered many more recorded harms from the homosexual parent. ... Thus, counter to the propaganda in reviews and professional associations' statements, it appears that children placed with the nonhomosexual parent in custody disputes by homosexual vs. nonhomosexual parents would have considerably less chance of being harmed or being exposed to harms and measurably reduced chances of living with a parent of inferior character as well. [*Id.* at 1193.]

22.   Many published studies purport to prove the negative proposition that there is no difference between parenting outcomes between same-sex and opposite-sex couples. It is theoretically impossible to prove the null hypothesis through social science methodologies.

23.   There are many published studies that state their conclusions more cautiously; they find a lack of evidence that the differences in parenting between same-sex and

opposite couples lead to any discernible differences in outcome. All of those studies are methodologically flawed and cannot reasonably be relied upon. Among the most significant flaws are inadequate size of the study population; use of self-selected study populations; and failure to use control groups. Those studies are summarized and critiqued in a recent article by George Rekers, Ph.D., and Mark Kilgus, M.D., Ph.D., professors at the University of South Carolina Medical School. *Studies of Homosexual Parenting: A Critical Review*, 14 REGENT U.L. REV. 343 (2002).

24.   The Rekers & Kilgus study finds the Cameron & Cameron Homosexual Parents study, *supra,* to be the least methodologically flawed. The sample size is the largest of any other study and there is a lack of bias in the random selection of persons to be interviewed. Rekers & Kilgus, *supra*, 14 REGENT U.L. REV. at 346, 355-359, 375, 380-381. However, because of "the small number of homosexual parents in that study ... their results [are] suggestive rather than conclusive. Their findings, however, indicate that the effects of homosexual parenting are still an open question, scientifically speaking, and warrant further research." *Id.* at 382. In conclusion, Rekers & Kilgus state:

> [T]he specific effect of homosexual parenting on child development remains an open question. Until methodologically rigorous research studies are conducted, empirical research has essentially nothing definitive to offer decision makers in child custody foster home placement, adoption, or artificial insemination cases. Until such sound scientific studies become available, such decision-making should remain in the realms of ethics, morality and law." *Id.*

25. The three learned articles referred to in this declaration are all reliable authorities within their respective fields of science and should be regarded as admissible evidence for purposes of Federal Rule of Evidence 803(18).

26. The sub-section of Mississippi Code § 93-17-3 that was passed in May 2000 has
        since been renumbered in 2006. The statutory section at issue is Mississippi Code

§ 93-17-3(5).

I declare under penalty of perjury under the laws of the United States that the foregoing is true and correct.

Executed this 14th day of October, YR-00.

Arvid K. Tolak, Ph.D.

Arvid K. Tolak. Ph.D.

M.F., et al.	)	
	)	
Plaintiffs	)	
	)	
vs.	)	Civil Action No. YR-00-3975
	)	
CHANCERY COURT OF VAN	)	
BUREN COUNTY, MISSISSIPPI, et al.,	)	
	)	
Defendants	)	

> UNITED STATES DISTRICT COURT
> **FILED**
> **October 21, YR-00**
> MIDDLE DISTRICT OF MISSISSIPPI

DECLARATION OF MURIEL ESTRADA GOMEZ, M.D., Ph.D.

I, Muriel Estrada Gomez, M.D., Ph.D., hereby declare as follows:

1. I am Vice President–Research of Highlands Pharmaceuticals, the fourth largest developer and manufacturer of pharmaceutical drugs in the United States. Highlands Pharmaceuticals is headquartered in Lofborough, Mississippi, and has research laboratories and manufacturing facilities in Lofborough as well as in several other locations in the United States and abroad.

2. My educational and professional background is as follows: I graduated *summa cum laude* from Millsaps College, in Jackson, Mississippi in 1977. In college, I majored in mathematics with a concentration in statistics and probability theory, and I minored in philosophy. I was elected to Phi Beta Kappa at the end of my junior year and was valedictorian of my class .

3.   Following my undergraduate education, I entered medical school at the University of California at Davis. While in medical school, I worked as a research assistant to three professors in the U.C. Davis Psychology Department. Their research required statistical analyses, with which I was able to assist them. Following my receipt of the M.D. degree in 1982, I completed the first three years of a residency in psychiatry, when I decided that my interests lay elsewhere.

4.   In 1985, I entered the Johns Hopkins University Bloomberg School of Public Health to study epidemiology. My special field of research interest was the epidemiology of sexually transmitted diseases. My Ph.D. dissertation was awarded the top prize for scholarly excellence in 1988. Following receipt of the Ph.D. degree, I remained at Johns Hopkins for eight more years as a research fellow and later as a member of the faculty of the Bloomberg School of Public Health.

5.   In 1996, I was recruited by Highlands Pharmaceuticals to become senior supervisor of epidemiological research. In 2000, I was promoted to my present position, Vice President–Research, where my responsibilities include overseeing all research activities of the company, with special emphasis on epidemiological, biochemical, and pharmaceutical research. I also coordinate the senior management team that is responsible for setting the company's long range research and development agendas. The opinions expressed in this Declaration are solely my own and do not reflect the opinions or viewpoints of Highlands Pharmaceuticals.

6.   Since, 1980, I have published (often with collaborators) over 250 scholarly articles in refereed journals in such diverse fields as epidemiology, psychiatry, psychology, sociology, and philosophy. In addition, I have published three collections of poetry and seven short stories of the medical detective variety.

7.   My primary field of scientific expertise is epidemiology. The nature of the field is well described in the following quotation:

> Epidemiology is the study of disease distribution and of the various determinants of health and disease risk in human populations. Epidemiologic methods are designed as means to gather unbiased evidence from groups of people in order to test hypotheses and to characterize the health of populations. Epidemiologic data provide a quantitative foundation for public health policy and clinical research, as well as a basis for preventive approaches in medicine and public health. [From the Bloomberg School of Public Health Web site at http://www.jhsph.edu/dept/EPI/.]

As can be readily seen, the research methodologies and analytical techniques of epidemiology have much in common with research and analytical methods in social psychology and other fields of social science.

8.   The attorney for the plaintiffs in this action have asked me to address the question of whether there is any scientific basis for the Mississippi statute that bars same sex couples from adopting children. My short answer is, there is not. They have also asked me to evaluate paragraphs 18-25 of the Declaration of Arvid K. Tolak, Ph.D., previously filed on behalf of the defendants in this action, and to express an opinion as to their scientific soundness. My short answer is that Mr. Tolak's statements and the articles on which they are based are scientifically unsound and that no rational decision maker would base a law or public policy upon them.

Paragraphs 18-19

9.   While I was at Johns Hopkins, through friends and colleagues at U.C. Davis, I met and became acquainted with the work of Professor Gregory Herek. Prof. Herek is an internationally recognized authority on prejudice against lesbians and gay men, anti-gay violence, and AIDS-related stigma. He has published numerous scholarly articles on these topics. His edited and co-edited books include *Hate Crimes: Confronting Violence Against Lesbians and Gay Men* (1992, Sage Publications), *AIDS, Identity, and Community: HIV and Lesbians and Gay Men* (Sage, 1995), *Out in Force: Sexual Orientation and the Military* (University of Chicago Press, 1996), *Stigma and Sexual Orientation* (Sage, 1998), and a special issue of the *American Behavioral Scientist* on "AIDS and Stigma" (1999). He is currently writing a book on sexual prejudice, which will be published by the University of Chicago Press. Professor Herek also serves as consulting editor for several academic journals, including Sexuality Research and Social Policy, Psychology of Men and Masculinity, Journal of Sex Research, and the Journal of Homosexuality. He has testified many times as an expert witness in cases involving stigmatization and legal disadvantages imposed on gay, lesbian, bisexual, and

transgendered people. Prof. Herek has taught me much about the scientific evidence relevant to this case, and I rely on what I have learned from him in formulating my opinions in this case.

10. In their submission to this court, the defendants rely on the published works of Paul Cameron and his associates. Tolak Decl. ¶¶ 18-21. Paul Cameron is no scientist. His writings are not relied on by the scientific community. Rather, his writings serve largely as sources of misinformation used by extreme right-wing anti-gay propagandists. Because he has been largely ignored by the scientific community, Cameron's works have not been subjected to published critiques in academic journals.

11. The most serious and substantial critique of Cameron's works was authored by Professor Herek and published in 1998. Gregory M. Herek, *Bad Science in the Service of Stigma: A Critique of the Cameron Group's Survey Studies*, in STIGMA AND SEXUAL ORIENTATION: UNDERSTANDING PREJUDICE AGAINST LESBIANS, GAY MEN, AND BISEXUALS at 223-255 (Sage Publ. 1998) (vol. 4 of Psychological Perspectives on Lesbian and Gay Issues, Greene & Herek ed.) (hereinafter referred to as *Bad Science*). Herek's *Bad Science* is a reliable authority and I am qualified to answer any questions about it.

12. In *Bad Science*, Herek gives a brief introduction to social science research procedures and vocabulary (beginning with probability sampling, convenience sampling, sampling frame, simple random sampling, and cluster sampling, and then the concept of validity). *Id.* at 226. Regarding sampling, he comments:

Because probability samples can be recruited in a variety of ways, researchers are expected to provide enough information about their methods in their published reports so that other scientists can replicate their procedures. However, details about sampling methodology have been sketchy or entirely absent from the Cameron group's published papers. [*Id.*]

He goes on: "Even if we assume that their study design met minimal requirements for recruiting a probability sample . . . three serious errors related to sampling issues are readily evident from their published reports." *Id.* at 227.

- *Error 1: Despite Their Characterizations of It, the Sample Was Not National . . .* "Even if the study were otherwise flawless . . . valid conclusions about the entire U.S. adult population could not be drawn from this sample. At best the findings could be generalized only to the populations of the eight municipalities" studied. *Id.*

- *Error 2: The Response Rate Was Unacceptably Low . . .* "[T]he Cameron group's results cannot be considered representative of even the specific municipalities [in which they gathered their data] because the vast majority of their sample did not complete the survey. . . . [A] high response rate is extremely important when results will be generalized to a large population. The lower the response rate, the greater the sample bias." *Id.* at 227, 228.

- *Error 3: Subsamples Were Too Small to Permit Reliable Analyses* . . . "The margin of error due to sampling decreases as sample size increases, to a point. For most purposes, samples of between 1,000 and 2,000 respondents have a sufficiently small margin of error that larger samples are not cost-effective. However, if subgroups are to be examined, a larger sample may be necessary because the margin of error for each subgroup is determined by the number of people in it. . . . Making estimates from a subsample of 17 [as the Cameron reports did] has an unacceptably large margin of error. In a simple random sample of 17, the margin of error due to sampling (with a confidence level of 99%) would be plus or minus 33 percentage points. . . . Thus, the confidence interval surrounding the Cameron group's proportion of 29% [of children of a homosexual parent who have incestuous relations with a parent] would range from at least -4% to +62%. This is such a wide margin of error that it is meaningless. Moreover, because the confidence interval includes zero, the Cameron group cannot legitimately conclude that the *true* number . . . was actually different from zero." *Id.* at 231-233.

Herek acknowledges that the majority of published psychological studies have similar problems. But "[i]s it possible that the Cameron group's studies, although not based on a representative sample, still offer valuable insights...?" Yes, he would say, but only if "their questionnaire and the procedures they used to collect data were valid," *i.e.*, only if they accurately measured what they were supposed to measure. *Id.* at 233. Prof. Herek concludes that they did not because of three additional methodological errors.

- *Error 4: The Validity of the Questionnaire Items Is Doubtful.* The questionnaire was so long that many respondents would tire and become careless before finishing. Yet the researchers included no systematic checks for internal consistency. The questions were often very complex. The questionnaire used language that was probably difficult for many respondents to understand. The questionnaire asked about highly personal and sensitive sexual issues. Many respondents might be inclined not to answer some questions truthfully. Yet the Cameron group did not employ any of the recognized techniques for minimizing lying and detecting when lying has occurred. Finally, some statements made by the researchers may have led some respondents to doubt that their answers were truly anonymous. In short, these and other failings "raise serious concerns" about the questionnaire's validity, "none of which were addressed in the Cameron group's published papers." *Id.* at 234-238.

- *Error 5: The Interviewers May have Been Biased and May Not Have Followed Uniform Procedures . . .* "To avoid systematic biases from interviewers' personal values or expectations, researchers typically employ field staff who are generally unaware of the study's hypotheses and who are carefully trained to communicate a nonjudgmental and respectful attitude to all respondents." *Id.* at 238. The Cameron group's published reports say nothing about training of staff or quality control. Of more serious concern, there is circumstantial evidence that one of the authors–perhaps Cameron himself–was directly involved in data collection for the 1983 survey." Yet the authors had clear expectations about the results, which were communicated to the pubic while data collection was in progress. They also had strong negative feelings about sexual orientation, revealed in their public statements at the time the surveys were conducted. *Id.* at 239-240.

- *Error 6: The Cameron Group's Biases Were Publicized to Potential Respondents While Data Were Being Collected.* While data collection was in progress, Paul Cameron was giving interviews to the press in or near some of the target cities. In one, "he was reported to have characterized the survey as providing 'ammunition for those who want laws adopted banning homosexual acts throughout the United States.'" At the same time, he was receiving "national attention for his calls to quarantine gays." *Id.* at 240.

Professor Herek concluded:

the multiple methodological problems evident in the Cameron group's surveys mean that their results cannot even be considered a valid description of the specific group of individuals who returned the survey questionnaire. Because the data are essentially meaningless, it is not surprising that the have been virtually ignored by the scientific community. [*Id.* at 241.]

Paragraphs 20-21

13. *Bad Science*, as summarized in Paragraph 8, *supra*, relates to the article referred to in the Tolak Declaration and to several spin-off articles therein cited. The second of the studies referenced by the Tolak Declaration, are Cameron's studies using a different data base. The series of studies exemplified by the articles referred to in the Tolak Declaration and written by the Cameron Group used as a data base information gleaned from appellate court opinions in contested child custody cases. The researchers endeavored through their search techniques to find as many cases of disputes involving couples consisting of one homosexual and one heterosexual. These cases were then matched to an equal number of cases of disputes involving couples consisting of two

heterosexuals. The opinions were then analyzed to discover specific harms suffered by the children of these couples, they were coded according to type of harm, and the two groups were compared with seemingly devastating results for the defenders of gay and lesbian parenting.

14. Neither common sense nor the Cameron group's reports offer any reason to conclude that the couples included in the sample selected by this method are representative of anyone but themselves. The selection of the samples was biased by self-selection. The couples in the sample would likely differ in meaningful ways from couples whose quarrels did not impel them to an appellate tribunal. The decision to appeal would bring into consideration the perceived stakes and risks in taking an appeal, financial ability to afford appellate litigation, the sense of righteous indignation that often drives a decision to appeal, the relative combativeness of the litigants as compared to couples excluded from the sample, and a host of other characteristics.

15. Cameron's assumptions about the high quality of the data to be gleaned from appellate court opinions are probably misguided for several reasons. First, a "harm" would become a data point for analysis only if it was mentioned somewhere in the appellate opinion. I am informed and believe that different courts have different traditions and practices of opinion-writing. In courts that believe that no fact should be mentioned in an opinion that is not relevant to the issues on the appeal, there would be a good chance that some harms would slip through the cracks. Whether they would mentioned in an opinion would depend on the fortuity of the legal issues that emerged from the couples' unresolved dispute.

16. The mere fact that a harm was mentioned in an opinion is not a reliable guide to whether the harm in fact occurred. The conclusion that a harm occurred because it was mentioned does not take into account such legal technicalities as the burden of proof and the standard of review on appeal.

17. Even if one only considered harms that were embodied in formal findings of fact, sometimes fact finders make mistakes. I am informed and believe that fact findings are often influenced by considerations other than the "truth," such as the lawyer's skill and attractiveness, the client's association with a dominant or stigmatized class, and exclusionary rules of evidence that are designed not to enhance the search for truth but to serve competing values such as efficiency or extrinsic policy. If evidence of harm does not emerge because a privilege blocked the testimony, that does not mean that the harm did not take place. If a litigant is so motivated by the stakes of the litigation and unresolved emotional issues with the ex-partner, the litigant may distort the truth with a strength of conviction far exceeding that of the subject of a questionnaire. Law and science have different motives and use different processes for attempting to find truth. The Cameron group's reports based on data gleaned from appellate opinions do not reveal

that any consideration was given to these differences. The fact that they regard appellate opinions as the "gold standard" for reliable fact gathering seems to be based more on myth than on a discerning grasp of reality.

18. As a scientist, I would regard it as completely irrational to rely on the Cameron reports based on appellate opinions as a source of information for differentiating home environments between heterosexual and homosexual persons.

Paragraphs 22-24

19. The Rekus and Kilgus article attached to the Tolak Declaration is not an example of reliable scientific literature. It is more likely a polished piece of persuasive writing. It was published not in a science journal but in a law review. I am informed and believe that law reviews do not have professional editorial boards and do not require peer review before a decision to publish is made. Peer review is an important mechanism for weeding out junk science. It is part of the dynamic process of hypothesizing, testing, replicating, falsifying, reconsidering, and publishing that is characteristic of the scientific enterprise. I am informed and believe that law reviews generally entrust to beginners in the profession the responsibility for selecting and editing the works they will publish. I suppose it is part of the teaching function of law schools to give students this heady experience. An article published in a typical American law review may be interesting, stimulating, or even provocative, but there is no requirement that it be reliable.

20. There is good reason to believe that the law review in which the Rekus and Kilgus article was published—Regent University Law Review—plays an advocacy role as to issues about law and homosexuality. Regent University was founded by Pat Robertson, founder of the Christian Broadcasting Network and a prominent national leader of the Christian right. Robertson continues to serve as Regent University's president. Robertson's views about the state of the law are well known. He issued a press release containing the following statements:

> [E]ven Jefferson could not have foreseen what the Supreme Court has done to the Constitution of the United States since 1962. Just think what five unelected judges have done to our nation's moral framework.
>
> In 1962, they ruled prayer out of the public schools.
>
> In 1963, they ruled the Bible out of public schools.
>
> In 1973, they applied a "right of privacy" not found in the Constitution as the basis for opening the door to the slaughter of more than 43,000,000 innocent unborn children.
>
> Subsequent federal courts have ruled the Ten Commandments were illegal in schools, that statues of Jesus were illegal in public parks, that prayers on a map in North

Carolina were illegal, and that it was illegal for little elementary school children to give thanks over their milk and cookies at snack time.

Now, the Supreme Court has declared a constitutional right to consensual sodomy and, by the language in its decision, has opened the door to homosexual marriages, bigamy, legalized prostitution, and even incest.

<http://www.patrobertson.com/PressReleases/supremecourt.asp>

21. The law school stresses its adherence to Christian principles:

The Regent experience is a meeting of minds and spirit - the Holy Spirit. There is purpose and empowerment beyond the academic instruction. Our students understand the meaning of being called by Christ.

<http://www.regent.edu/acad/schlaw/welcome/home.cfm>

22.   Regent's Mission Statement reiterates that adherence and exudes a spirit of missionary zeal:

The mission of Regent Law School is to bring to bear the will of our Creator, Almighty God, upon legal education and the legal profession. In particular, this mission includes:

- The education and training of students to become excellent lawyers within the standards of the legal profession.

- The grounding of students in biblical foundations of law, legal institutions, and processes of conflict resolution; recognition of questions of righteousness in the operation of law; and pursuit of true justice through professional legal service.

- The nurturing and encouragement of students to become mature Christians who exercise the gifts of the Holy Spirit and display the fruit of the Holy Spirit in their personal and professional lives.

- The nurture and encouragement of other law students, practicing lawyers, judges, legislators, government officials, educators and others to recognize and seek the biblical foundations of law, to recognize questions of   ·   righteousness in the operation of law; and to pursue true justice.

<http://www.regent.edu/acad/schlaw/welcome/mission.cfm>

23. The Rekus and Kilgus article was published in the Regent Law Review as part of a symposium entitled "Homosexuality: Truth Be Told." Excerpts from the blurbs describing the articles in the symposium leave no doubt as to the role of the symposium as a work of advocacy. Consider the following:

- Child Molestation and the Homosexual Movement, by Steve Baldwin, addresses several recent *attacks on our society driven by the homosexual movement.* From the international campaign to lower or remove age of consent laws, to the recent assault on the Boy Scouts of America, *homosexuals are waging an all out campaign to normalize homosexuality.*

- Crafting Bi/Homosexual Youth, by Judith Reisman, exposes *fraudulent sex scientists and sex education*; and discusses the power and effect the media and gay rights organizations have on "turning" children gay. This articles presents undeniable proof that homosexuals are after the hearts and minds of the nation's children.

- Selling Homosexuality to America, by Paul Rondeau, explores how *gay rights activists* use rhetoric, psychology, social psychology, and the media–all the elements of modern marketing–to position homosexuality in order to frame what is discussed in the public arena and how it is discussed.

- Gay Orthodoxy and Academic Heresy, by Ty Clevenger, reveals the controversy behind the Stanford Law & Public Policy Review's rejection of every article that questioned or criticized *orthodox gay rights views.*

- Defending Marriage: A Litigation Strategy to Oppose Same-sex "Marriage", by Dale Schowengerdt, suggests strategies that may be employed by those seeking to *defeat the homosexual lobby in order to uphold the traditional view of marriage.*

<http://www.regent.edu/acad/schlaw/academics/lawreview/issues/v14n2.html> (Emphases added.)

24. Recently published research literature increasingly avoids many of the methodological limitations of earlier studies, and they continue to confirm the consistent findings over time that the outcomes of adoptions by homosexual couples are not significantly different from the outcomes of adoptions by heterosexuals. As an example, one may review an article by Susan Golombok, et al., *Children With Lesbian Parents: A Community Study*, 39 DEVELOPMENTAL PSYCHOLOGY 20 (No. 1, 2003). This methodologically sophisticated study leads the authors to the following conclusion:

Research on lesbian-mother families has broader implications for increasing theoretical understanding of the role of parents in children's psychological development in general. For example, the findings of the present investigation suggest that the presence of two parents irrespective of their gender, rather than the presence of a parent of each sex, is associated with more positive outcomes for children's psychological well-being than is rearing by a single mother. That is, it may be the involvement of a second parent rather than the involvement of a male parent that makes a difference.

It also appears that maternal sexual orientation is not a major influence on children's gender development because boys and girls in lesbian-mother families were not found to differ in gender-typed behavior from their counterparts from heterosexual homes. This finding, obtained from a representative sample of children with lesbian parents using a measure that was specifically designed to assess within-sex variation in gender role behavior, is of particular interest given the suggestion by Stacey and Biblarz (2001) that possible differences in gender development among children of lesbian mothers may be under emphasized by researchers in this area. From a theoretical perspective, this contradicts the view that heterosexual parents are essential for children's acquisition of gender typed behavior. [*Id.* at 31.]

See also Charlotte J. Patterson, *Gay Fathers*, ch. 14, in THE ROLE OF THE FATHER IN CHILD DEVELOPMENT 397-416 (Michael E. Lamb ed., John Wiley & Sons, 2004).

25. The Golumbok et al. and Patterson articles described in the preceding paragraph are both reliable authorities, and I am qualified to answer any questions about them.

I declare under penalty of perjury under the laws of the United States that the foregoing is true and correct.

Executed this 21st day of October, YR-00, in Bethesda, Maryland.

Muriel Estrada Gomez
Muriel Estrada Gomez, M.D., Ph.D.

Natalie Moldonado
485 Court Street
Lofborough, MS 38706
Telephone: (756) 922-3828

Attorney for the plaintiffs M.F., C.W. & K.G.

In the

UNITED STATES DISTRICT COURT

FOR THE MIDDLE DISTRICT OF MISSISSIPPI

M.F., et, al.	)	
	)	
Plaintiffs	)	
	)	Civil Action No. YR-00-3975 MT
vs.	)	
	)	
CHANCERY COURT OF VAN BUREN	)	
COUNTY, MISSISSIPPI, et. al.	)	
	)	
Defendants	)	

NOTICE OF APPEAL

Notice is hereby given that plaintiffs in the above-named case, M.F., K.G., by her next

friend, C.W., and C.W. on her own behalf, hereby appeal to the United States Court of

Appeals for the Thirteenth Circuit from the final judgment entered in this action on the

23rd day of November, YR-00.

Dated: December 5, YR-00.

Respectfully submitted,

Natalie Moldonado

Natalie Moldonado
Attorney for the plaintiffs M.F.,
C.W. & K.G.

CERTIFICATE OF SERVICE

I certify that on this 5th day of December, YR-00, I served the foregoing Notice of Appeal upon the defendants by causing a copy thereof to be mailed, first class postage prepaid, to the attorney for defendants, Gavin Peter Hess, Deputy Attorney General of Mississippi, Mississippi Attorney General's Office, State Justice Building, 450 Broad Street, Jackson, MS, 39201.

Natalie Moldonado

Natalie Moldonado
485 Court Street
Lofborough, MI 38706

Attorney for the plaintiffs